W9-BCG-808

Leadership for Youth Ministry

A resource developed by the
Northeast Center for Youth Ministry

Saint Mary's Press
Christian Brothers Publications
Winona, Minnesota

Cover design by Carolyn Thomas.
Acknowledgments continue on page 165.

ISBN: 0-88489-157-7

Leadership for Youth Ministry

Contents

Introduction

If you are a youth ministry leader, you were not born that way. Some of you were drafted, some volunteered, some were trained, and some of you are paid for your work. There is a remarkable variety among you as leaders, but you all share something in common: by whatever path you arrived, you are now key figures in the Church's presence to young people.

As youth ministry leaders, you face a significant challenge. Today, youth ministry is broadly conceived as the pastoral ministry of the Church to young people—not only spiritual, but also educational, social, relational, and catechetical. It is complex, holistic, and exciting. It requires that we, as a Church, move beyond narrowly focused leadership roles. In youth ministry, as in the other pastoral ministries, there is an active search for a leadership model that is faithful to the gospel and responsive to the times. This book has been written as a contribution to the search.

If you share responsibility for some part of a parish youth ministry program, this book is for you. It is especially suited to your needs if you *coordinate* these programs, whether you are a paid youth minister, a member of the pastoral staff, or a committed volunteer. Also, we think this book would be valuable to you if you are a diocesan staff member who is expected to advise and train parish youth ministry leaders.

The topic of this book is well suited to the main work of the Northeast Center for Youth Ministry, namely, the development of effective leaders for youth ministry at the parish, school, or diocesan level.

From our observations and experience, we have formed a clear point of view on the roles and functions of youth ministry leaders. We have also gathered together the principal theories and tools that are most useful in training programs. In this book, we share with you these resources and concepts. Whether or not you completely agree with our presentation, we hope you will find it thought-provoking, clarifying, and practical. This book has been written to be of service to the youth ministry practitioner. It reflects our belief that when we take time to widen or deepen our understanding, we also strengthen the quality of our ministry.

Just as the concert performer is spotlighted by the meeting of different beams of light, youth ministry leadership is examined in this book with the aid of several disciplines—management science, pastoral theology, psychology, applied behavioral science, and adult education. Not all of the concepts will be new to you, but what may be original is the synthesis of these diverse perspectives to obtain a better grasp of the nature of youth ministry leadership.

The chapters of the book have been organized into three parts.

Part One, "A Framework for Leaders," sets out the assumptions that guide the book. It provides an overview of leadership theory and its implications for youth ministers.

Part Two, "Leadership Roles in Youth Ministry," moves into a more detailed description of the responsibilities of youth ministry leaders. It makes important distinctions among the functions of coordination, team leadership, and program leadership.

Part Three, "Leadership in Action," contains more immediately practical chapters on how to conduct planning sessions, organize volunteers, and support new leaders. Worksheets and resource references accompany various chapters of the book.

May youth ministry prosper!

The Northeast Center Staff
Zeni Fox
Marisa Guerin
Brian Reynolds
John Roberto

Part 1

A Framework for Leaders

1
Ministry and Leadership

Any discussion of youth ministry in the contemporary Church must first focus on the evolution, or perhaps explosion, of all ministries. It was not so long ago that ministry was the sole responsibility of bishops and clergy, who ministered *to* the people. Vatican II began the theological and pastoral shift toward a broader understanding of Christian ministry. We shifted our focus to a community understanding of ministries — in which ministries arise out of all the gifts distributed among all the people. Ministries became ministries *of* the people. This evolution in our thinking results from sound scriptural and historical research, as well as a renewed theology of Church. For the past two decades this theological evolution of our concept of ministry has brought about several very significant shifts in emphasis. James Coleman, SJ, describes them very well when he writes:

> The adoption of "ministry" language has gradually shifted several important priorities in possession a decade ago. For example, the appeal of the language of ministry assumes that baptism takes priority of eminence over ordination. It is the most basic and fundamental sacrament, the ultimate justification and source for all further sacraments, including ordination. Second, the term, ministry, as it is being used presupposes a theology of charisms by which plural and different gifts are distributed freely by the Spirit within the community. . . . Note how in this view charism takes priority over office. Office is in the service of the charisms.
>
> Again, those who speak of ministry tacitly assume by the language that emphasis should be placed on skills, accountability, and competence. . . . Function and competence take precedence over a professional clergy determined by status as ordained . . . ascribed status yields to achieved status. Finally, the appeal to ministry language masks a collegial, a non-collegial, monarchial and purely hierarchial model. To speak of ministry is to evoke this whole gestalt of the priority of baptism, charism, competence, and collegiality over ordination, office, status, and hierarchy.[1]

Youth ministry, in its growth and development, has been part and parcel of this shift in emphasis. *A Vision of Youth Ministry*[2] grew out of the theological and pastoral developments of the post–Vatican II Church. The growth of the professional lay coordinator of youth ministry attests to the shifting priorities in ministry and church. The leadership given by adult and youth leaders who are responding to their baptismal call to share the gifts the Spirit has blessed them with is the true measure of the impact of our new consciousness of ministry has brought upon us.

These signs of growth have also brought new responsibilities upon those in leadership. Thomas Groome has identified the question of criteria for ministry as a central responsibility for those in leadership. Groome writes:

1) All ministries require some explicit recognition and delegation by the Christian community.
2) The would-be minister must have the aptitude, interest, and ability for the particular ministry to which he or she is being called.
3) The person, in addition to personal aptitude and ability, must have adequate preparation for his or her ministry.[3]

These challenges require new skills for the leader. As we explore more deeply the nature of leadership—its functions, roles, theories, and skills, it will be important to keep in mind the ministry consciousness which has given rise to the new role of the leader in Christian ministry, and especially in youth ministry.

The Scope of Youth Ministry

While it is not the purpose of this book to describe the concept of youth ministry, it is necessary, at least, to reflect on the scope that it embraces. *A Vision of Youth Ministry* gives two goals for youth ministry:

1) Youth ministry works to foster the total personal and spiritual growth of each young person.
2) Youth ministry seeks to draw young people to responsible participation in the life, mission, and work of the faith community.[4]

These goals are far-reaching; a brief reflection on them suggests the broad effort they point toward:

- "Personal growth" suggests the developmental tasks of adolescence, the implications of the social scientific research on the needs of adolescents, the multiplicity of dimensions of the personality that are to be nourished.
- "Each young person" calls to mind the intellectually gifted and mentally retarded, the college-bound student and the potential dropout, the handicapped, the sports star.
- "Spiritual growth" requires growth in all dimensions of faith: cognitive, affective and behavioral, requiring opportunities for study, prayer, liturgical celebration, and service to others.
- "Participation in the life, mission, and work" implies active roles, both leading and following, and therefore the creation of those roles and the training needed to fill them effectively.

Another way of focusing on the breadth of effort the *Vision of Youth Ministry* calls for is to consider the components of youth ministry which it outlines. Since "youth ministry is the response of the Christian community to the needs of young people, [as well as] the sharing of the unique gifts of youth with the larger community," the components of youth ministry indicate that using a holistic approach may best meet the needs of young people. A brief examination of the components suggests the variety of programs that an approach rooted in the needs of youth will engender:

Word: Faith is a treasure, and young people need opportunities to hear the Good News (evangelization), to reflect on its meaning in their lives (catechesis), and to grow in the ability to share it with others (mission).

Worship: Youth need to lift up their lives to God. They need opportunities for prayer, liturgical celebration, retreats, and they need help to grow in their ability to worship in various ways.

Creating Community: For relational ministry to occur, youth need to form personal relationships with each other and many adults in the community. The initial level of involvement is marked by friendliness, calling people by name. In time, and with commitment, the possibility for deeper relationships, for faith-sharing, and for mission-sharing, evolve.

Justice and Service: A response to the Good News of God's love for us is love for our neighbor; therefore, opportunities for this response are part of youth ministry. Such opportunities might include service to others in the local and world community through group and individual activities, and activities planned to help effect greater justice in various human organizations.

Guidance and Healing: Some youth have particular needs — such generally recognized needs as those of delinquent and alienated teens, drug- or alcohol-dependent youth, and runaways, as well as the less visible needs of the lonely, those suffering because of family troubles, and the insecure. All need the care and concern of interested adults and other teens.

Enablement: To effect the various dimensions of youth ministry, knowledge and skills are needed. Leadership training of various kinds, for teens and adults, helps to build a total youth ministry.

Advocacy: The task of addressing the larger adult community about the needs of youth and calling for the programmatic response that is required to meet those needs is generally performed by adults on behalf of teens. This advocacy is also a component of youth ministry, for many other components often depend on the success of adults speaking on behalf of youth.

It is helpful to focus on the goals and components presented in the *Vision* statement, because they suggest the growth needed in every church in order to effectively serve the needs of youth and enable youth to share their gifts with the larger community. In every community they present an invitation to expand the opportunities for youth ministry. They also suggest the need for many leadership roles in a vital, local youth ministry.

Leadership Roles in Youth Ministry

The leadership of youth programs poses questions for parishes as the field of youth ministry develops. The very term *youth minister* can mean professional or volunteer, coordinator or specialist, depending upon the background and assumptions of the parish leaders.

Throughout this analysis it is well to bear in mind that we are dealing with a structure and a reality that is not yet fully formed. Expectations vary greatly as to what a church's youth ministry should accomplish, what kinds of programs it should include, what methodologies it should utilize. Hence, expectations of what youth ministers should do also vary greatly.

An easy contrast can be drawn by thinking about the roles in a Catholic high school—such as principal, department chairperson, janitor. Over the course of time a highly differentiated assortment of roles has evolved in the school; the school structure is clearly defined. While expectations still vary about the specifics of performing the roles in question, the general definition of what the principal does and what the janitor does is set, the lines of accountability are drawn, the content and often the procedure for evaluation are determined. In most church settings, a look at the role of the youth minister shows that the situation is markedly different: there is little definition of what is to be done, there are unclear lines of accountability, and ways to evaluate content and procedure are uncertain.

It is important to recognize that when we talk about youth ministry, in many churches we are talking about efforts to evolve new positions, new structures. In this book we are presenting our vision of how youth ministry could develop, outlining our sense of what the positions, the structures, and the programs in the local church could be. We hope, of course, that this vision will contribute to the evolution of a more clearly defined youth ministry in the larger Church.

It should also be noted that what leaders (and followers) do in youth ministry in the course of the next several years will help to shape the positions and the structures of youth ministry efforts. In this way, they will help to shape the expectations of church members for youth ministry. Therefore, it is important that leaders and churches be intentional about the structural ramifications of their day-by-day efforts.

The chapters in Part Two will analyze the leadership roles in a youth ministry program and the functions that need to be performed to develop a comprehensive youth ministry program. The presentation will be both descriptive (what is done) and prescriptive (what needs to be done). We invite an active participation by the reader in both of these dynamics: analyzing his or her present situation and determining what is needed for growth in that situation.

In the next two chapters, the principal dynamics of leadership and a psychological perspective on personal styles are developed to serve as a framework for understanding youth ministry leadership.

Notes

1. James Coleman, "The Future of Ministry," *America,* 28 March 1981.

2. *A Vision of Youth Ministry* (Washington, DC: United States Catholic Conference, Department of Education, 1976).

3. Thomas Groome, "Signs of Hope: The Diversification of Ministries," *PACE* 12, DIRECTIONS-A.

4. *A Vision of Youth Ministry,* p. 4.

2
The Dynamics of Leadership

Leadership Theories

Paul, the youth minister at St. Malachy's Parish, was leaving his position after establishing an exceptionally successful youth program there. A party was held in the church hall to thank him for his years of service to the community. Clusters of people filled the room, celebrating their appreciation and affection for him and feeling a bit sad and anxious at the prospect of his leaving. One woman said to her husband, "He's so special, a real leader. I hope the next youth minister is, too." But she shook her head doubtfully. In another conversation, an earnest young man was sharing his opinion with the parish DRE. "I worked on the retreat team with Paul and I really appreciated his collaborative way of organizing things. If all Church leaders had that style, we'd be better off." Perched on a nearby windowsill, one of the juniors in the youth group confided to her best friend, "You know, Paul really helped me grow up. When I was a freshman I was such a troublemaker! But this year I organized the food drive all by myself. He sure went through a lot with me!"

These comments reflect certain assumptions that many people have regarding leadership. The first assumption is that leadership is a trait, a characteristic that some people are born with. The woman who perceived Paul as a special sort of person had some doubts about whether the new youth minister would have "it"—that inborn ability to be a leader. However, the trait theory of leadership is a static one that does not allow room for growth. Some people certainly are gifted with leadership talents, but most people have to *learn* leadership.

Another assumption that many people have about leadership is the behavioral theory.

Like the earnest young man, people with this assumption believe that different people have different leadership styles and that there is a universal "best" style of leadership from among these types of leaders—authoritarian, democratic, laissez-faire, and shades in between. They believe that if all leaders used the one "right" style, we would have fewer problems.

Can that be true? Notice, the young man applauded Paul for having an open, collaborative style of leading the retreat team. However, if he had been a youth group advisor, perhaps he would have observed that Paul behaved in a more authoritarian manner when he disciplined troublesome freshmen. And yet, Paul respected the older youth leaders enough to let them handle their own projects by themselves—a laissez-faire leadership style. So which style is best?

The answer is "It depends." The behavioral theory about leadership has to give way to one that is capable of greater adaptability. Situational Leadership is the name for that more dynamic conception of the leadership function. According to this theory, developed by Paul Hersey and Kenneth Blanchard,[1] leadership style has to combine properly with the specific situation and with the condition of the followers in order to function effectively. More than likely, Paul's success as a youth minister was due to his accurate perception of the best leadership style to use in different situations and his skill in using the various approaches.

Leadership, defined situationally, is "a process of influencing the activities of a person or group in efforts toward accomplishing goals in a given situation."[2] Several key aspects of youth ministry leadership are implied in this definition.

The leader is one who serves. The particular leadership activities of the youth minister are determined by the needs and objectives of the youth ministry program he or she is working with. This concern for the real-life conditions of a parish or school anchors the ministry leader in fidelity to the community. The principle of leadership as service means that the leader performs an "unblocking" role, anticipating and facilitating solutions to the group's difficulties as it goes about accomplishing tasks.

Leadership can be learned. Since many styles of leadership are needed for different aspects of a youth ministry program, leaders will be more gifted at some leadership styles than others. No one person will be equally gifted for every situation. Better leadership skills can be fostered if the youth minister takes stock of the talents that come naturally and bolsters these with skills that must be acquired. For example, the leader who is a good troubleshooter and dependable in a crisis may complement that talent by working on the skills of planning in advance, making lists, and keeping organized. On the other hand, the person who is naturally highly organized may need to practice ways of making people feel welcome or valued. It feels awkward to learn new skills, but practice brings greater ease. The effectiveness of a youth ministry leader may depend on how broad his or her behavioral repertoire becomes.

Leaders are recognized by their followers. Given the definition of leadership from Hersey and Blanchard, simple authority or power will not go very far. The influence that comes from being an officially designated leader— associate pastor, DRE, professional youth minister—can be a valuable help as the leader establishes credibility, but eventually the leadership has to be recognized as such by the followers. Without that perception the youth ministry leader has limited influence. In fact, groups can and do make life difficult at times when they feel controlled by someone who has power, but who is not serving them with leadership.

Situational Leadership

Extensive research in human relations has documented that the functions of a leader fall into two broad categories: *task behavior* and *relationship behavior.* Briefly put, task behavior encompasses all that the leader does in order to get the work of youth ministry accomplished. It involves knowing what youth ministry is all about, how to organize and carry out programs, what responsibilities must be handled, who is in charge, when and where things are to be done, and how to enable other people to assume leadership. A person's task orientation may be high or low. High task behavior is quite directive and exercises a significant influence over what is being done. Low task behavior is not apathy or disinterest, but a lower involvement with the question "What is to be done?"

Relationship behavior—the second broad category of all leadership functions—is the process of supporting and facilitating co-workers in their interactions around the task. For the youth ministry leader, this means giving verbal affirmation, communicating clearly, encouraging volunteers, listening to their concerns, helping to resolve conflicts, and showing interest. Like task behavior, relationship behavior can be low or high.

For some time it was thought that task behavior and relationship behavior were found on opposite ends of a continuum, and that a person's leadership style would fit somewhere along this line.[3] However, further research confirmed that these two functions are independent of one another, and can be found in any combination. In other words, there are persons who exhibit a high task orientation coupled with a low relationship orientation, and vice versa. Yet there are also persons who are high in *both* task and relationship behavior, or *low* in both. The unique insight of the Hersey/Blanchard situational leadership model is their point that one person can learn each of those four styles, and use them appropriately according to circumstances.

Let us take a closer look at how these various styles are used by Carmen, the youth minister at Holy Savior Parish, located downtown in a large city. Over the summer months, Thursday night was an evening for volunteer youth to come and work on the new youth drop-in center at Holy Savior. There was painting to be done, fix-up work, carpeting, and the setting up of a game area, music equipment, and so on. On Thursday nights Carmen could be found lining up the evening's chores, assigning them to the work crews that showed up, checking their work, answering questions, and generally keeping things hopping. When their energy wore down she raided the icebox for cold drinks and congratulated the teens on their evening's work.

Carmen was exhibiting the High Task-Low Relationship style of leadership called *directing*. She was knowledgeable and focused on getting the evening's work done, but she also paid some attention to the group's need for affirmation.

On another occasion during the fall, Carmen spent an evening facilitating a group meeting of the social action committee. The adults and youth on this committee were working on a project to raise awareness and money for the hunger problem—an issue to which they all felt committed. In the course of the meeting Carmen facilitated the agenda, gave the quieter members opportunities to have their say, made encouraging suggestions, kept the conversation on track, and in general contributed fully. Her style that evening was High Task-High Relationship, called *coordinating*. She was combining directive task behavior with active attention to the feelings and needs of the group.

Several of the adults from that meeting were also involved in the parish retreat planning team. The retreat leaders had done the planning process several times before and were comfortable with the task. When she met with them, Carmen showed a Low Task—High Relationship style called *collaborating*. She was affirming and interested in the group, but they basically conducted the planning with minimal direction from her.

The fourth style of Low Task-Low Relationship, called *delegating,* is the one that characterized Carmen's leadership of the youth gospel choir. This was a stable group with a trained volunteer leader. The group was experienced and motivated and it contributed to the life of youth ministry at Holy Savior with a fairly low level of task or relationship behavior from Carmen.

Carmen's experiences demonstrate why Hersey and Blanchard also call their situational leadership theory a "life cycle" theory of leadership. They feel that the appropriateness of the different styles is determined by the life cycle stage of the follower group. They maintain that every new group or new task presents the followers with a journey of maturity. It may take them one week or one year to manage that journey, according to the complexity of the challenge. Basically followers must grow in the *ability* and *knowledge* they need to do the task, and in their *willingness* or *motivation* to do it well. Thus, a "low maturity" work group does not mean that the persons are immature, but only that they do not yet have the knowledge or interpersonal harmony they need to do the job independently.

The examples from Holy Savior reflect groups with increasing levels of task-relevant maturity: the teen construction crew, the budding social action committee, the more experienced retreat leaders, the highly independent gospel choir. The sequence of leadership styles that matches this movement from low to high group maturity follows the styles Carmen used: directing (High Task-Low Relationship); coordinating (High Task-High Relationship); collaborating (Low Task-High Relationship); delegating (Low Task-Low Relationship).

An interesting dilemma confronts most youth ministers who encounter this theory of leadership. When they test themselves for style preferences (see

Resources on Situational Leadership at the end of this chapter), they usually discover that they are best at the two very relational styles—coordinating and collaborating. Only a minority of the youth ministers tested thus far are really comfortable with the two low relationship styles of leadership, directing and delegating.

This means that many youth ministers are at a disadvantage when they are dealing with groups that are either very low in maturity or very high. A confident directing style is most helpful, for example, when there are disciplinary problems in a newly forming youth group, or when a new group of adult volunteers is gathered together and wants to know what they are supposed to *do* (not how they feel about one another). At the other end of the spectrum, problems with mature followers can arise because the high relationship youth minister is not very comfortable with delegation. This not only frustrates competent co-workers, but it can also block the full development of youth or adult leaders being recruited and nurtured by the youth minister.

Of course, there are competent and effective youth ministers who feel more gifted at getting things done than building relationships. For these leaders the weakness may lie in moving too quickly from a directing style to a delegating style, without spending enough time providing encouragement, a listening ear, and advice. The temptation is to delegate quickly to a volunteer who seems to have the right talents. Unfortunately, the volunteer often ends up feeling stressed or taken for granted, unless he or she has received adequate personal support.

Learning the skills to expand a youth minister's range of leadership styles is not necessarily difficult, but it can be experienced as a threatening challenge. Many youth ministers who are "relationally gifted" like to have that style returned to them. They may be afraid that being less relational and more directive will cause them to lose the affection or admiration of their followers. Their reluctance to delegate may come from a fear of not being needed. More task-oriented youth ministers may balk at the time-consuming aspects of the relationship styles.

The sense of threat, however, is far outweighed by the advantages of a more flexible leadership style. Paul, the youth minister we met as he was leaving St. Malachy's, had reaped the benefits of his good leadership. He had also given a rare gift to his parish: the sensitive care of a leader who was able to diagnose the needs of his followers and respond to them.

Summary

Kurt Levin, a pioneer in group dynamics, once said, "There is nothing so practical as a good theory." Theories are the beliefs and assumptions that guide actions. In this chapter, we have reviewed the development of three leadership theories: the trait theory, the behavioral theory, and the situational leadership mode.

The four kinds of leadership behavior described by the situational theory are directing, coordinating, collaborating, and delegating. For the youth minister, this model provides a way of analyzing his or her leadership style patterns. It is a model that helps leaders to match certain kinds of behavior to different situations.

The next chapter complements this theory by introducing the perspective of psychology.

Resources on Situational Leadership

Hersey, Paul, and Kenneth Blanchard. *Management of Organizational Behavior.* Englewood Cliffs, NJ: Prentice-Hall, 1982.

Leader Effectiveness and Adaptability (Lead) Instrument, as well as related handouts and instruments, can be ordered in the *Situational Leadership Sampler* from Learning Resources Corporation, 8517 Production Avenue, P.O. Box 26240, San Diego, CA 92126.

Notes

1. Paul Hersey and Kenneth Blanchard, *Management of Organizational Behavior* (Englewood Cliffs, NJ: Prentice-Hall, 1982).

2. Ibid., p. 83.

3. Robert Tannenbaun and Warren H. Schmidt, "How to Choose a Leadership Pattern," *Harvard Business Review* (March–April 1957): 95–101.

3
A Psychological Perspective

In the last chapter we looked at leadership styles as they apply to different situations. In this section we will focus on the leader as a person with a particular configuration of personality traits and, therefore, with a particular gift for leadership. The framework for this analysis will be the Myers–Briggs Type Indicator.

The Myers–Briggs Type Indicator

Carl Jung, the early student of Freud who subsequently developed his own system of psychological thought, published a theory of psychological types. Katherine Briggs, and subsequently her daughter Isabel Briggs Myers, accepted this theory and used it to systematize their own observation of different kinds of people. In time they developed a questionnaire, the Myers–Briggs Type Indicator (MBTI), in order to determine key aspects of personal preference. This instrument has been used widely, in different countries and with different groups of people.

The MBTI measures basic differences in the way people prefer to use their minds. Carl Jung identified two kinds of mental functions: *perceiving* and *judging*. Perceiving is the process of becoming aware of the world and ourselves in it. Judging is the process of coming to conclusions about the world and ourselves, based on what was perceived. Behavior flows from the judgments that are made, which depend on what was perceived. This means that understanding preferences in the area of judging and perceiving helps us to understand different styles of behavior.

In Jung's theory, there are two ways of perceiving: one directed toward the outer world, one to the inner. The first is *sensing*, becoming aware of the world through the use of the five senses; the second is *intuition*, a perception based on the use of the unconscious, becoming aware of the ideas and possibilities that it suggests. The MBTI measures a person's preference for exercising one of these perceptions more than the other. Each preference is viewed as a valid and good one, simply different from the other. The same is true with the preferences discussed below.

There are also two ways of judging. The first, *thinking*, utilizes a logical process; the other, *feeling*, is based on appreciation. The focus of thinking-judging is impersonal, based on data, consistency, and logic. The focus of feeling-judging is personal, based on valuing and on subjective factors like "pleasing-ness" and "fitting-ness." The MBTI also measures a person's preference for using one of these methods of judging over the other.

In addition to naming these basic processes, Carl Jung discovered that an individual has greater interest in either the outer or the inner world. A person who prefers to focus on the outer world of people and things exercises *extroversion*; someone focused on the inner world of ideas and concepts exercises *introversion*. These preferences, also, are measured by the MBTI.

A final set of preferences is seen in relation to the *perceiving* and *judging* functions themselves. One is the dominant, preferred function, shaping the primary attitude toward life. The second is the auxiliary function, at the service of the first. This is the final preference which the MBTI measures.

The various combinations of these four preferences give rise to sixteen basic types. When each preference is assigned a letter, E(xtroversion)—I(ntroversion); S(ensing)—(i)N(tuition); T(hinking)—F(eeling); J(udging)—P(erceiving), the following chart can be drawn:

| | | SENSING TYPES | | INTUITIVES | |
		Thinking -ST-	Feeling -SF-	Feeling -NF-	Thinking -NT-
Introvert	I—J	ISTJ	ISFJ	INFJ	INTJ
	I—P	ISTP	ISFP	INFP	INTP
Extrovert	E—P	ESTP	ESFP	ENFP	ENTP
	E—J	ESTJ	ESFJ	ENFJ	ENTJ

There is value in understanding one's own type for the sake of personal insight and a better understanding of one's own gifts. Furthermore, an understanding of the effects of the preferences the MBTI measures can help the leader understand others better. Finally, his or her type can also tell an individual a great deal about personal leadership style. Each type has particular strengths and weaknesses; more importantly, each type has particular gifts. Isabel Myers begins her book with the following quotation from Saint Paul:

> For as we have many members in one body, and all members have not the same office: So we, being many, are one body . . . and every one members of one another. Having then gifts differing. . . .
> (Romans 12:4–8)

The list of resources at the end of this chapter contains references to the most readily available tests that can be used to determine one's type.

Description of the Personality Types

1) *Extroverted Thinking Types (ESTJ and ENTJ)*
Because these types turn attention to the outer world and use an analytical, impersonal approach, they are natural organizers and strong executives. Their preference for the judging function causes them to make decisions easily. Truth is very important to these types, as are facts and rules. Feeling and perception are less important. When the auxiliary function is sensing, this type is matter-of-fact and practical. When the auxiliary is intuition, they are interested in new possibilities, in problem-solving, and in long-range possibilities.

2) *Introverted Thinking Types (ISTP and INTP)*
In contrast to the extroverts, these analytical types focus attention on the inner world, hence on underlying principles. Because they are perceptive in relation to the inner world, they are generally reserved and detached. If the auxiliary function is sensing, this type may organize ideas, or be involved in practical and applied science. With the intuitive as auxiliary, the individual focuses on theory and abstract thought and, perhaps, is involved in research.

3) *Extroverted Feeling Types (ESFJ and ENFJ)*
The dominant trait, feeling-judgment, with the focus on the external world, gives these types great interest in people and in their responses. Warmth and acceptance are their desire, both given and received; harmony is of central importance. The dominant judging factor makes them decisive and orderly. With sensing as an auxiliary, it indicates traits such as matter-of-factness and practicality; when intuition is the auxiliary, it indicates traits like vision, insight, and imagination for new possibilities.

4) *Introverted Feeling Types (ISFP and INFP)*
These feeling types focus attention on the inner world, placing the greatest emphasis on personal values. Because the outer world is less important to them, they often do not express their inner convictions and feelings. In dealings with the outer world, they are open-minded and adaptable with little need to impress others. When sensing is the auxiliary, this type has a clear sense of the needs of the moment. A preference for intuition, on the other hand, makes the companion type able to deal with possibilities.

5) *Extroverted Sensing Types (ESTP and ESFP)*
With these types the five senses are used to gather information about the external world. This gives them a keen sense of realism and practicality. Because their dominant trait is perceiving, they are adaptable and tolerant. They enjoy life, and learn primarily from their own experience. When supported by thinking, this type has a greater awareness of underlying principles

and anticipated outcomes. Being perceptive, this type is friendly, tactful, and interested in people.

6) *Introverted Sensing Types (ISTJ and ISFJ)*

The five senses are again important, making these types both practical and painstaking. However, because they deal with the external world with their judgment faculty, they tend to be hard working and very responsible. When the judgment is by thinking process, this type is analytical and decisive. When it is by feeling process the emphasis is, instead, on loyalty and consideration.

7) *Extroverted Intuitive Types (ENTP and ENFP)*

The dominant perception of these types is possibilities, all different kinds of possibilities, in the external world. Their driving force is inspiration, leading them to original viewpoints, many projects, and the possibility of inspiring others. When supported by thinking, this type is analytical and impersonal in their relationships with people. With feeling as the auxiliary, this type is interested in people and works well with them.

8) *Introverted Intuitive Types (INTJ and INFJ)*

Again, these types focus primarily on possibilities, but their introversion makes them very individualistic. The judgment that they exercise in relation to the external world causes them to be determined, often having a great deal of drive. With the support of thinking, the intuition is used for innovation and reorganizing and solving difficulties. When feeling is the supporting function the intuition is utilized to understand people and to work for or with them.

Types and Leadership

Each of the types described can make a contribution to leadership, although some types will do so more easily, and each will be more effective in different aspects of the leadership task. For the extrovert, the task of leading others comes more naturally and is easier to achieve. However, the introvert's reflection on ideas and concepts can contribute to the kind of vision a leader holds up for others to follow. Intuitives see the possibilities—new ways to do things, new ways of using the gifts of others. But the sensing types see more clearly what needs to be done, what is already there, and what is lacking. The thinking types are best able to analyze and develop a plan; the feeling types are best able to involve people in carrying out the plan. Those whose dominant function is a judging one are good at getting things done; when the dominant is a perceiving function, they are good at seeing clearly what needs to be done and bringing a sense of enjoyment to it.

There are two points to ponder in relation to the MBTI and leadership. First, the value of each person's gifts must be appreciated. Without the perspective offered by Carl Jung's theory, there is a strong tendency for people to devalue or think poorly of those whose type is different.

For example, let us look at Sharon and Bob, both involved in the youth ministry planning team at Our Lady of the Sea Parish. Sharon's preference is for the judging function (J) and Bob's is for the perceiving function (P).

Sharon, with her ordered and well-planned way of living, has a tendency to regard Bob as unreliable or capricious. For his part, Bob with his open and flexible way of living, has a tendency to think that Sharon is rigid and only half alive. When they are at meetings together their different styles are only too evident. Sharon wants to pin down all the details of an upcoming program and Bob wants to leave things loose enough so that he will be able to respond to the actual situation when it is happening.

When the youth ministry team at Our Lady of the Sea took the Myers–Briggs Type Indicator and discussed it together, Sharon and Bob realized that their conflicts came from their opposite strengths. Neither one was an incompetent youth minister; in fact, they were very good at their own style of dealing with programs. The MBTI helped them to realize that they could maximize each other's gifts by learning to rely on Sharon for advance planning and to rely on Bob for on-the-spot troubleshooting. With their improved teamwork, their mutual respect grew.

The second point to consider regarding the MBTI and leadership is related: the effective leader draws on the gifts of many people for a more complete leadership system. At Our Lady of the Sea Parish, the work of the youth ministry team was coordinated by Father Vince, the associate pastor. Father Vince's type was ENFJ. With the insight provided by the discussion that he had with the other members about the MBTI, Father Vince came to realize that there were no members of the team with a preference for the sensing mode of perceiving (S). That fact helped to explain why the team found it so tedious to keep track of some very important realities, such as their program supplies and their budget. Father Vince promptly recruited several volunteers who were gifted in their ability to manage resources, and the team's overall effectiveness showed a noticeable improvement.

Summary

Self-knowledge is the key to growth. In this chapter the personality theory of Carl Jung and the insights provided by the Myers–Briggs Type Indicator have been used to illustrate the rich diversity among people. For youth ministry leaders, self-knowledge can bring confidence to the exercise of their gifts, as well as respect and openness to others when styles come into conflict.

This psychological perspective builds on the situational leadership theory presented in chapter 2. Together they provide a framework that leaders can use to guide their attitudes and behavior toward others.

Resources on the Myers–Briggs Type Indicator

Hogan, R. Craig, and David W. Champagne. "Personal Style Inventory." In *1980 Annual Handbook for Group Facilitators*. San Diego: University Associates, 1980. Write to: University Associates Inc., Box 26240, 8517 Production Avenue, San Diego, CA 92126.

An article containing a questionnaire for determining type, description of the dimensions of the typology and an overview of the strengths and weaknesses of the types. (The authors give permission to reproduce for educational, training and research activities.)

— Keirsey, David, and Marilyn Bates. *Please Understand Me*. Del Mar, CA: Prometheus Nemesis Books, 1978. Write to: Prometheus Nemesis Books, P.O. Box 2082, Del Mar, CA 92014.

Book with a "Temperament Sorter" questionnaire to determine type and detailed portraits of each type. Examines implications in the areas of mating, child-rearing, and leadership (including education).

"Myers–Briggs Type Indicator"—test forms, answer sheets, and explanatory booklet, available from Consulting Psychologists Press, Inc., 577 College Avenue, Palo Alto, CA 94306.

Myers, Isabel Briggs, and Peter B. Myers. *Gifts Differing*. Palo Alto, CA: Consulting Psychologists Press, Inc., 1980. Write to: Consulting Psychologists Press, Inc., 577 College Avenue, Palo Alto, CA 94306.

Book giving an overview of the types utilizing much of the research that has been done with the Myers–Briggs indicator. Draws out practical implications of type and work settings, in marriage and in educational settings.

Part 2

Leadership Roles in Youth Ministry

As the field of youth ministry grows, it is accompanied by new questions about the responsibilities of those who lead youth programs. The term *youth minister* contributes to the creative confusion, since there are many different definitions for this role.

At the present time, the term *youth minister* is used in two ways, describing either a particular position or those performing a particular pastoral task. When it is used to describe a position, the responsibilities of that position vary greatly. Sometimes, there is an unspoken assumption that the youth minister is *the* person responsible for working with the youth in the church. If the individual minister holds this assumption, he or she will engage in an individualistic ministry. In its best form this results in the appearance of a charismatic leader; unfortunately, more often the individualistic assumption produces the negative result of a "Pied Piper" or "guru." If the church members hold the assumption that the youth minister is the only one responsible for the youth, they may resist the efforts of the youth minister to draw many members of the community into ministry with youth. They may ask, "Why did we hire, appoint, and commission him (or her), anyway?"

At other times, the youth minister is seen as the person responsible for providing leadership for youth ministry in the local church by working with youth and adults. It is this description of the position of youth minister that we will be using in this book.

The term *youth minister* is also more generally used to describe all those people who are performing a particular pastoral task, namely, ministry to, with, by, or for youth. In this sense, just as there are many catechists in a vital religious education program, there are many youth ministers in a vital youth ministry program. This book will also examine the implications of leadership concepts for those performing various dimensions of the pastoral task that is youth ministry.

4
The Coordinator of Youth Ministry

The Task

Youth ministry is a concept that embraces all of the many ways that the faith community responds to its youth. It is not a single program, but a variety of programs that are united in a common philosophy and purpose. In effect, the many programs that a parish may sponsor provide opportunities for ministry to occur. As programs designed to meet the needs of youth multiply, coordination of the parish's efforts becomes essential.

Coordination is defined as "the act or state of working together or functioning in harmony." The essential task of the coordinator of youth ministry is to facilitate the harmonious working together of the various programs that embody the Church's youth ministry efforts. This involves both a visionary and a practical dimension. At the level of vision, the coordinator helps the parish community to define its mission in relation to youth, its statement of purpose, and goals in youth ministry. At the practical level, he or she keeps lines of communication and planning open so that parishioners understand how individual programs are related to the Church's mission statement and to other programs.

The task of coordination also involves the development of new programs that may help the local church to achieve its mission more effectively. In addition, coordination meets the Church's need to relate the efforts of the local church with that of the broader community, both secular and ecumenical, and with the larger Church, including the vicariate and the diocese.

Concretely, what might the coordinator's calendar include in a given week in the spring? Perhaps a meeting with the youth ministry council (the adults and youth who developed the mission statement) to evaluate the effectiveness of a recent retreat. Maybe a talk to the parents of the Confirmation students to explain the youth ministry program for the following year. In a large town, perhaps a meeting with youth ministers of several of the other churches to begin planning an ecumenical prayer service to be conducted by youth on the Fourth of July. Possibly, attending a diocesan in-service day on new catechetical materials. Or a supper with two program leaders who are scheduling events not included on the cooperative youth ministry calendar. Maybe a report to the parish council on the proposed outreach program for teenagers at the new detox center.

It can quickly be seen that these responsibilities do not primarily involve the coordinator in direct work with youth. That does not mean that a coordinator of youth ministry might not also lead a youth group meeting, coordinate a car wash, or teach a class during this spring week, but only that these additional tasks are not part of the *coordination function.*

The preceding description of the task of youth ministry coordination raises several questions: When is this role needed? Who can or should fulfill this role? What background or experience is needed to function effectively in this role? How has this role emerged in actual parish situations? What difficulties arise in undertaking this task? How can difficulties be met?

Let us explore these questions more closely.

The Role

When is the role needed? In one sense, this question could be answered "always." Part of the coordinator's task includes leadership in developing programs to meet the needs of youth. When a comprehensive youth ministry effort has not yet begun, the development need is great. However, in many parishes the development of youth ministry is not begun by someone filling the coordinator role, but rather by diverse youth ministry leaders beginning different programs. Ideally the role is always needed, but actually the need for it is often discovered gradually, as youth ministry grows. Once a parish has begun to offer a variety of programs for youth it is essential that someone take on the role of coordinating these efforts.

Who can or should fill this role? The actual answer to this question varies from parish to parish (after all, leadership is situational). These answers, therefore, are all conditional ones. A professional youth minister could fill the role. Indeed, if a youth minister is hired, generally he or she would do so. However, some youth ministers do not want the role and do not have the skill needed for it. Their expertise lies in the actual implementation of programs with youth, rather than in the area of coordination. In those cases careful consideration must be given to who could perform the coordinator task. A pastor could assume the role, or assign it to an assistant pastor; each would probably delegate some aspects of the task to others. A DRE or other pastoral minister could assume the coordinator role, especially if he or she had the particular skills needed for the task. However, it would be difficult for a parish volunteer to fill this role, because volunteers generally lack the legitimacy that is needed to exercise authority in performing the task, both within the parish and beyond it. The answer to this question, then, depends on the parish and the people staffing it.

What background experience is needed? The coordinator of youth ministry needs an understanding of youth ministry and of the scope of his or her leadership role. The coordinator needs skill in the leadership functions that were described in chapter 1: planning, enabling leadership, training leadership. He or she needs skill in working with groups, including an understanding of group dynamics and of conflict management. Time management would be another needed skill.

Pastoral Examples

How has the role emerged in actual parish situations? Three examples will show the existing diversity and suggest the possible direction for a particular local church:

St. Claire's is a large suburban parish. For many years it has employed two DREs who coordinate an elementary and high school religious education program, as well as planning adult education programs. Competent professional women, the DREs recognized that the high school religious education classes were not meeting all the needs of the youth. Serving as advocates for youth to the pastor and parish council, they proposed that the parish hire a youth minister to develop a youth ministry.

Marie was employed the first year for ten hours a week. She worked to get to know the young people and to start a youth group, serving as its leader. The religious education program continued as before. The second year Marie was employed for twenty hours a week, the third year full time. As the position evolved she involved adults and youth in varying leadership roles, including a youth ministry planning team; she assumed responsibility for the high school religious education program; she developed new programs in the areas of service and guidance; and she began participating in diocesan youth ministry meetings. In short, she gradually assumed the role of coordinator of youth ministry.

As Marie's role expanded, her title did not change. In her case, the time spent did change. If she had originally worked full time a similar growth could have occurred by the gradual delegation of certain program-level tasks as she assumed new tasks at the coordination level. Marie gained perspective on how to expand the youth ministry effort by studying for her M.A. and by talking with other youth ministry leaders in the diocese. Growth occurred in both Marie and in youth ministry in the parish.

St. Joseph's is a large, semirural parish. The adults of the parish have long shown a vital interest in their youth. Volunteers developed many kinds of programs for the teenagers, encouraged by a kindly, laissez-faire pastor. A group of men ran an extensive sports program; a number of Marriage Encounter couples conducted very successful in-home fellowship groups; the Knights of Columbus sponsored a Squires Group devoted to serving the needs of the parish. In addition to their efforts, Denise, the DRE, organized a religious education program for high school students. Many youth were involved in these different programs.

Denise attended a youth ministry workshop, and in assessing the parish's youth ministry efforts she realized that youth were not involved in leadership roles, and that there were various needs of many youth that were not met. She decided to begin a youth ministry council, inviting representative youth and adults from all existing groups to an initial meeting. In addition to facilitating the growth of the council as a planning and coordinating group, Denise initiated some new program efforts. As she did so, she gradually assumed the role of coordinator of youth ministry, sharing that task with the youth ministry council. This became a dimension of her work as DRE.

St. Gabriel's is a large, city parish serving an Hispanic community. When Father Joe was assigned there he found there were no activities for youth. Over the course of several years he invited many adults and youth to begin various programs: a sports program, a Daughters of Mary, a religious education program, a service club. He also began sending teens to the diocesan-sponsored retreats, took a group to the CYO convention to determine if they would like to begin a teen club, and hosted the vicariate youth ministry planning day. In fact, Father Joe assumed the role of coordinator of youth ministry from the beginning of his assignment at St. Gabriel's although he never considered it that, let alone used the title.

Challenges

What difficulties arise in undertaking this task? How can they be met? There are probably as many answers to this question as there are parishes. However, we will examine some common areas of difficulty, including the problem of change, the question of legitimacy, people's perception of what ministry is, and their perception of who is responsible for it.

The problem of change

Various books have been written about change and the planning of change. One basic perspective they all share is that most people initially resist change. This means that the effort to move toward a new youth ministry role and to develop new ways of ministering to and with youth generally incurs resistance. In the examples given above, Marie encountered resistance from the pastor in expanding her role to include a sex education program, and Denise encountered resistance from leaders of the various programs to beginning a youth council. In each case it took about a year of discussing the idea before beginning implementation. (Needless to say, much patience is needed in this process.)

To deal with the problems of change, the first step is to understand the normal human reaction to change. The second step is to develop some strategies for facilitating the acceptance of the coordinator role. Helping others see the need, enlisting them to help develop the plan, and selling the idea to all involved are some helpful ways to reduce the time it will take for the change to be accepted.

The question of legitimacy

Legitimacy is the perceived right to exercise authority. Father Joe, a parish priest, encountered little difficulty in beginning new programs at St. Gabriel's because his authority was easily accepted by the people. Furthermore, the programs he began did not represent a change in what people expect the church to offer, as a draft-counseling program might have done. When Marie worked as the youth group leader her authority was accepted because she was the officially designated youth minister. Her role in directing the high school religious education program was more difficult, because the catechists questioned her legitimacy in relation to that of the DREs. They perceived the DREs as both more trained and more experienced, and in addition felt personal loyalty to them. In the second parish example, Denise encountered much resistance from the youth ministry leaders because they questioned what right she had even to convene them, let alone to coordinate their efforts.

To deal with this effectively, it helps to seek ways of "being legitimized." One youth minister reported that when she introduced new ideas she had learned at the diocesan seminary, they were more readily accepted than similar ideas of her own. A volunteer who was named youth minister found that he had more acceptance than he had previously, even though he was doing the same tasks. A new youth minister who worked closely with the parish team had much early success, in part because the pastor was perceived as sharing his authority with the youth minister. Yet another volunteer, hired by the parish as youth minister, found that her acceptance in the secular and ecumenical community was greatly enhanced.

The perception of ministry

The perception of what ministry is, including youth ministry, presents another area of potential difficulty. In some cases the parish's perception may be that ministry is what the officially designated ministers (the staff) do. In that case, they resist involvement. Marie found that in her first year no adults would share leadership in the youth group—"After all, that was why we hired you."

In other cases, the individual's perspective may be that ministry is a one-on-one relational task. From that point of view the role of coordinator and the tasks that go with that role are not considered to be *real* ministry.

Also, the community's understanding of who is responsible for ministry affects what occurs. A careful examination of the language used earlier in the chapter to describe the coordinator of youth ministry role will show an underlying presupposition that the ministry belongs to *the community*. Therefore, the coordinator facilitates the community's definition of its mission, harmonizes the efforts of the community's leaders, and assists the community in evaluating the effectiveness of the youth ministry effort. Unfortunately, sometimes individuals—both staff and volunteers—act as though the ministry were theirs, especially when introducing new ideas. Failure to involve the community in the decision-making process is a sign of this, and so is the appearance of the "guru" style in a youth minister.

At other times, the community acts as though the ministry belonged to an individual, especially when evaluating the youth ministry effort. Blaming the individual—even when a major part of the problem is lack of involvement of the adults of the community—is an indication of this.

Changing the perception of ministry, both of what it is and whose it is, is a gradual process. In the parish it means fostering understanding of the Church as the People of God, and of ministry as the work of that people in response to God and to others. In some communities this still represents a new perspective, and one that will only be learned slowly. Behavioral change helps understanding, so gradual involvement of people in youth ministry efforts (especially when utilizing their particular gifts and talents) will be important. A liturgical celebration to affirm the youth ministry leaders in a ceremony patterned on those now used in many parishes on Catechetical Sunday, would contribute to this understanding. The "coordinator" dimension would evolve slowly in such a setting.

In relation to the individual leader, a process of reflecting on the meaning of servant leadership would help change perceptions. Two points in particular could be meditated upon. First, servant leadership is at the service of the community; the community is the focus, not the individual. As one wise pastor would say, "They must increase, I must decrease." Second, servant leadership considers both gifts and needs. So the individual asks, "What gifts do I have, and therefore, what can I do in this community?" But just as important a question is "What are the needs of this community and how can I call forth the ministerial gifts of others to help meet those needs?" Such a perspective recognizes with Paul that "in the Church there are many different kinds of spiritual gifts, but the same spirit gives them. There are different ways of serving, but the same Lord is served. There are different abilities to perform service, but the same God gives ability to everyone for their service." (1 Cor. 12:4–6) The role of coordinator *is* a vital ministry, just as much as the more relational roles of teacher, guide, and advisor.

Summary

The role of coordinator of youth ministry is the linchpin that maintains harmony in the total youth ministry effort of a parish. Without this coordination youth programs tend to be fragmented and many new opportunities are missed. However, the coordinating role does not have to be filled by a full-time youth minister. It can also be covered by another member of the parish staff or by a duly appointed volunteer.

The thoughtful exercise of the coordination function can be a major support for ongoing youth ministry, but it is not an easy role to introduce. The parish must come to terms with its understanding of ministry and must be willing to give legitimacy to the youth ministry coordinator.

The coordination function is one of the three basic types of leadership roles in youth ministry. The next chapter will analyze the second leadership role, that of the youth ministry team member.

5
The Youth Ministry Team

The Task

In the Church today collegiality is an important concept which we are still striving to embody in parish structures. Collegiality implies a sharing of power and authority, a sharing of decision-making and the tasks of implementation—a working together. One expression of collegiality is team ministry.

Parish team ministry has been tried by some staffs, with varying ways of defining the idea in practice. Thus, various types of youth ministry teams have evolved. They have in common the effort to conduct work together, the effort to be collegial. The actual work varies. Sometimes a team coordinates the total parish effort, with all members equal in decision-making and in the carrying out of the work. At other times, a team works with a coordinator of youth ministry, especially in the planning and evaluation processes for the total youth ministry effort. Some teams work in only one dimension of youth ministry, such as a religious education program or a retreat program. Their work is closer to that of "youth ministry program leaders," and will be treated in the next chapter. In this section, teams of the first two types described above will be discussed.

The Role

The same questions that were raised in the last chapter can be asked again in respect to a youth ministry team.

When is the role needed? Remembering the three parish situations described briefly in the last chapter, only St. Gabriel's did not involve some type of team. And only at St. Gabriel's was a priest the coordinator. Some studies in situational leadership help to shed light on why this might have been so.

One study is that by Fred Fiedler.[1] He holds that three variables influence leadership style: leader-member relationships (good or poor), task structure (structured or unstructured), and leader position power (strong or weak). Depending on the configuration of these three variables, Fiedler holds that either a task-oriented style or a relationship-oriented style of behavior will be more effective.

It is hoped that in a youth ministry effort, *leader-member relationships* will be good; in the parishes we described they were at least basically positive. Most often, the *task* is still relatively unstructured, as was the case in these examples. (By contrast, consider the working of a school where schedules, testing procedures, registration procedures, hiring procedures, and so on are all very structured.) However, in most situations the *leader position power* will vary greatly. It will depend on such factors as the role of the person (the role of priest has more position power than that of DRE); their status (the priest DRE has more position power than the lay DRE); the individual's age, education, and length of time in the role; and various other factors involving the group's perception of the leader.

Fiedler would say that, given good relationships and an unstructured task, a leader with strong position power could function well with a task-oriented style, primarily directing others in what they should do. Father Joe did this. A leader in a similar situation, but with weak position power (Marie, a new youth minister, or Denise, turning to youth ministry for the first time) would function better with a relationship-oriented style. That style would lead to developing a structure in which other people took part in decision-making and sharing power with the leader. Both Marie and Denise, in fact, did this.

Fiedler's analysis, then, indicates that in many situations a leader needs a team in order to function optimally. Another factor that points toward the need for a team is the availability of time. In the long run, team ministry makes more efficient use of time, even though at the point of initiation team ministry takes more time. This early investment of time is required because people have to be invited to be part of the team; they have to learn as much as possible about youth ministry. Also, they must build community, both to model the nature of ministry and to work more effectively together. A consensus decision-making mode in the group is also more time-consuming than if one person makes the decisions. However, at the point of implementation a team both shares the work to be done and advocates for its importance in the broader community, so that implementation of the various programs takes less time and shares the task more equally.

The nature of the planning process presents a third reason for considering a youth ministry team. A key principle of good planning is: "Involve those you are planning *for* in the planning process." Having members of the parish, both adults and youth, be part of the team can result in programming which more faithfully serves the needs of the community. Various parts of the planning process, such as analysis of local needs and decisions about the best time for programs, can be facilitated by the presence of those whose needs are to be met.

The person responsible for the youth ministry in a parish must assess these various factors and determine whether a youth ministry team is needed. Then that individual, alone or with the team, must determine the scope of the team's task, whether it will be total coordination, or planning and evaluation, and so on. The question of who is responsible to whom (lines of accountability) must also be considered along with the scope of authority the team will exercise.

So, for example, the pastor may decide to delegate responsibility for total coordination of the youth ministry effort to a team, who are to be accountable to him and the parish council with a semiannual evaluative report, stipulating only that they work within the confines of the budget developed by the council. He may have decided to do this for several reasons. He may not have time to oversee the effort himself (for example, as coordinator of the team), or there may be several strong leaders he thinks can do the job well, or he may believe that such a structure best exemplifies the collegial model he is attempting to embody in his parish.

Similarly, the youth minister might decide that he or she wishes to develop a council to work with in planning and evaluation. The reasons might be that he or she is new and young (weak position power), unfamiliar with the parish (in need of help with the planning process), and presently overwhelmed with the task since all services to youth have long since died (task unstructured, lack of time).

Who can or should fill the role? This question can be answered in three ways: in terms of the team members' personal characteristics, their roles, and their ages. Let's consider age first. Some teams have been made up only of adults; others consist only of youth, except the youth minister. What will actually work in a particular situation does vary, but ideally speaking, a team that includes both youth and adult members is best. Including youth is a way of fulfilling a goal of youth ministry, namely, drawing young people into responsible participation in the life, mission, and work of the Church.[2] It is also faithful to the principle of involving those to be served in the planning process. Finally, the leadership role of young people models to their peers their value and place in the Church.

However, adults also play an essential role on the team. They bring greater life experience and personal maturity to the task. Often they are able to serve on the team longer, giving stability. (Teens graduate and move away.) They play an important role in the planning process because they represent others whose needs are met in a total youth ministry. the parents, the priests, and the whole community, who have a responsibility for handing on the faith to the next generation. They are able to give greater legitimacy and more active support in the parish to the youth ministry effort.

Some of the essential characteristics of team members would include an active faith, a willingness to work on behalf of youth, and a willingness to work as a member of a team. Special gifts like a sense of humor, practical prayerfulness, capacity for envisioning ways of building the kingdom in this place, a loving heart, and skill at listening could all be sought for a balanced team.

Another consideration has to do with the roles the team members already hold. For example, in Denise's situation as described above, she first invited the adult leader and a youth representative from every parish program serving youth. It was probably necessary that she begin that way, but in fact most of the adults did not come back after the first meeting. It took time to find a representative from each group with that key characteristic: willingness to work with a group. In Marie's parish the work of her council would probably have been facilitated if she had asked one of the DREs to make a one- or two-year commitment to serving. In both examples the issue is representation from parish groups serving youth.

A second aspect of role has to do with the informal leadership various teens exercise in their respective groups: parish, neighborhood, or school groups. Consideration should be given to the types of informal groups that exist in the parish—the athletes, the studious types, the good-time crowd, the alienated. Inviting leadership from several of these groups helps to keep the team representative. Similarly among the adults, it is important to have parents included, and they should also be representative of various viewpoints in the parish (i.e., liberal, conservative).

It may sound as if a very large group is needed for the team. Actually, when choices are made carefully each person probably represents several groups. A team of six to fifteen is possible; a team of eight to ten is generally most manageable.

What background or experience is needed? Initially, all team members should have sufficient leadership qualities in order to demonstrate that they will be able to function effectively in their role. Additional knowledge and skills can be developed through a training program. The training should include an overview of youth ministry, should recommend resources for the team to work with so that they can understand the needs of youth, and should teach some approaches for meeting those needs. Also, skills needed to perform the task they have been assigned should be taught, including planning and evaluating skills. Many of these skills are presented throughout this book.

For the most part the real expertise of the team will develop as they work together. They will expand their knowledge and skill by evaluating their successes and failures, by taking opportunities to talk with teams in other parishes, by attending workshops, and by reading articles. And as they work and learn, they will embody that which youth ministry will become.

Pastoral Examples

Two typical examples were described in the preceding section, St. Claire's and St. Joseph's. Two other ways that teams develop are illustrated by St. Joanna's and Sacred Heart.

Shortly after he was ordained, Father Jack came to St. Joanna's—a large, city parish. He believed strongly in collegiality in the Church and had read several books about program planning. He decided to begin a youth ministry team that would work with him in all dimensions of developing a comprehensive youth ministry. He assessed the parish carefully and in January invited several persons who had the requisite leadership capacity to join the team. These included teenagers and young adults.

With them he attended a day-long youth ministry workshop. Then he invited a trainer to lead the group through a program planning process over a period of several months. Part of the process was devoted to team-building activities with the group. By May they were ready to announce a series of celebratory year-end activities for the youth in June, a summer theater program, and the outline of a fall youth group program. As teenagers flocked to the first programs the team knew it was off to a good start.

At Sacred Heart, a group of parents who were involved in the charismatic renewal began to discuss the lack of opportunities for teenagers in their parish. They decided to work together as a team to plan meetings of teenagers in their homes, and with the consent of the pastor began a very successful program which they planned together and took turns leading.

After two years, team members Irene and Dick decided to take a series of courses in youth ministry in order to help themselves and the other adult leaders to be more effective. As they learned more about the diverse needs of youth and reflected on the small proportion of the parish youth then involved, they realized that a more comprehensive youth ministry effort was needed. They began the process of educating the rest of the team to this need, thereby gradually bringing the team from one that led a single parish program to one that advocated and began to plan a more comprehensive effort. Theirs eventually became a team ministry in the sense we have described, and expanded the opportunities for youth ministry at Sacred Heart.

Challenges

What to do first? The first challenge is the time that it takes to develop a team. Note that at St. Joanna's it took six months for a team to form, to plan, and to announce its first activities. In the earlier examples, Marie and Denise took about a year to get their councils established. (Their lower position power in comparison to Father Jack's would have been a factor in this.) Those attempting the development of a team need to be aware of this, lest they give up too soon.

When a person first assumes leadership in relation to a youth ministry program, he or she may not be able to put primary energies into beginning a team. Sometimes people in the parish take a "wait and see attitude" or want some immediate results. This is a real dilemma for the leader. Marie's strategy was to first get the youth group started; a year later she began to develop a council. On the other hand, Father Jack began by developing the team first. Each strategy had positive and negative results.

The person new to the primary leadership role in a youth ministry program has to consider the alternatives: whether to first develop a team to plan with, or to first "do something." One way to help resolve the question of what to do is to refer to the assigned job description. Another way is to assess one's personal position power, and decide if it is strong enough to effect such a change immediately — knowing that those who need a team most have weak position power, but also knowing that it takes a support group to effect change!

Whatever strategy is used first, a process of educating the larger community (parish staff, council, committee, and parish as a whole) should be undertaken. The process should communicate what is now being done and why, and what will need to be done later and why. The language chosen for reports, talks, bulletin announcements, and newsletter contributions should help educate the parish to the needed strategies.

Close community or closed community?

Another difficulty can be seen by looking at the later history of youth ministry at St. Joanna's. For two years programs involved many youth, but then numbers began to shrink. After four years only a handful of youth were involved. Why did the numbers of teens involved shrink so dramatically?

(It's important to say here that this does not mean to imply that numbers make success. However, a variety of diverse programs serving different youth is a general indication that there are many opportunities for ministry. Multiple ways of serving the needs of many youth is an indicator of a healthy and comprehensive youth ministry program.)

One explanation lies in the nature of the team and the planning dynamic. From learning and working together the initial team became a close community. (There was no change in membership, as high school graduates in this area continued to live at home, whether they commuted to work or to college.) In group settings they more and more related with each other, and less and less reached out to newcomers and alienated young people. They began to be perceived as the "in-group," and others felt like outsiders. Furthermore, when they assessed needs and interests they spoke only from their own experience, which in turn was shaped by the leadership training and spiritual development programs they had been part of as a team. They understood primarily the needs of those seeking to be part of the mission of the church, and not those whose needs were fellowship, evangelization, and catechesis. The result? The programs they planned did not meet the needs of most teenagers at St. Joanna's.

An added factor contributed to this difficulty: the youth ministry effort lacked the active support of parents — and older adults in general — in the parish. They were not part of the planning process, and so had neither input nor a sense of ownership of the program. Furthermore, no effort was made to explain to them why the youth ministry efforts had evolved programs like a summer theater and a graduation picnic. While they were not opposed to such activities, parents did not feel they were essential and, therefore, did not give often-needed encouragement to their teenagers to become involved.

St. Joanna's illustrates the need for understanding group dynamics. Many parishes have experienced this difficulty, wherein the core group becomes *the* group. The formation of a close community can lead to a closed community. Especially with teenagers and young adults who are still seeking their identity, a close community can be very important, and "outsiders" can represent a threat.

One strategy that can allay this problem somewhat is to plan that only two or three team members be present at most programs, especially in a visible leadership role. Secondly, whenever possible, additional leaders from the program area should be called forth, trained, and given roles in that area, along with or instead of team members. (The coordinators and planners need not be the implementors.) Finally, the team members should reflect on this question: How might they deepen both their own group life and their presence to the larger community?

The situation at St. Joanna's also points to the need to involve many people in the planning process, as was discussed above. The absence of parents and older adults on the team contributed to the problem in two ways: Their needs were not met in the program, and their support was not enlisted.

Traditional leadership

Difficulty sometimes arises regarding the authority of a youth ministry team to provide leadership. This is particularly true when there is a change in the staff person responsible for youth ministry, whether pastor or youth minister. At times the new staff member does not favor a collegial style or wishes to limit the authority of the team. At times the team is unwilling to accept leadership from someone new, especially if the team was called forth to ministry by the previous staff member.

When a staff member who has worked with a team or who has delegated authority to a team leaves, both the new staff member and the team should be aware that it is a crisis point in the life of the team and the parish. Both parties to the situation, the individual and the team, must work patiently and prayerfully to evolve a new group life. For the new staff member a dedicated and competent team is an invaluable resource for ministry. Even if he or she wishes to gradually change the type of involvement or the authority given the group, this should be done with care and consideration, for these are fellow ministers who have served the church. For the team, the new staff member may be the designated authority in relation to the group, and therefore, has an important role to play and gift to contribute. Even if the old leader is sorely missed, the new one less congenial, and the question of the team's future authority uncertain, patience and caring must be exercised.

In such situations it would be important that both parties discuss openly their evaluation of what has come before, and their expectations for the future. If it would be helpful, other leaders could be called upon to help evolve a new group life, for example someone from the diocesan office or someone who has made a similar adjustment. Gradually the "new" team will come to life.

Narrow focus

Another source of difficulty arises from choosing a team to coordinate a comprehensive youth ministry entirely from people involved in a single program. Whether this be high school catechists and religious education leaders, or teen club officers and advisors, or youth and adult retreat leaders, the dynamic tends to be the same. Rather than evolving a more comprehensive youth ministry with diverse components, they strive to add new dimensions to their existing program. So the religious education group may decide on a service project for the students, the teen club group may determine that new officers should go to a leadership training program, and the retreat leaders may elect to begin a junior high retreat. For the most part this has the effect of limiting new efforts only to those youth who are already involved in a particular program. It is very unlikely, for example, that youth from the other programs will assist in the service project, or that youth retreat leaders would learn about the leadership training event. This limits the comprehensiveness of a parish's youth ministry.

To guard against this possibility the youth minister should strive for a representative team, not one from a single program area. Furthermore, a new mix of people with different perspectives enriches the pool of fresh ideas — especially relevant in the brainstorming and strategizing work of a planning group.

It is safe to say that the basic step in meeting all of these difficulties is realizing that the development of a team takes time, effort, patience, and prayer.

Summary

The youth ministry team represents a way of exercising leadership in a parish which can greatly enhance the vitality and scope of the parish youth ministry. Different gifts and leadership styles can be utilized by involving several persons on the team. With more people to implement ideas, more can be done. Mutual support and encouragement can be given by team members to each other.

However, at the present time teamwork is still more an ideal in the Church than a well-established, tried-and-true mode of operation. Learning to be a team will occur as individuals strive to work cooperatively together. Motivation will increase as the fruits of teamwork are experienced.

The final leadership role, that of the youth ministry program leader, will be presented in the next chapter. The program leader's relationship to the coordinator of youth ministry and to the youth ministry team will be seen.

Notes

1. Fred E. Fiedler, "The Contingency Model: New Directions for Leadership Utilization," *Journal of Contemporary Business* (Autumn 1974): 66ff.
2. *A Vision of Youth Ministry*, p. 4.

6
Youth Ministry Program Leaders

The Task

In the last two chapters we have presented two roles that provide leadership for the total youth ministry effort of a parish: the coordinator and the youth ministry team. In addition to these comprehensive coordination and planning tasks, a third important task faced by the community is providing leadership for the various program areas. Program areas are as diverse as sports, religious education, service activities, social events, and retreats. In each of these program areas there is obviously a need for leaders who will coach, teach, guide, or chaperone. But those functions are program implementation roles—unless someone also takes on the specific leadership task of planning, enabling, and training volunteers for these programs, they will flounder.

The Role

By now, it should be evident that the pattern in this book is to present the leadership *tasks* very clearly, but to be very flexible in describing how the roles should be filled. This is quite intentional; the operating principle is "form follows function." Rather than making absolute statements, such as "Every parish should hire a full-time youth minister," it seems more appropriate to present the kinds of responsibilities that are the heart of youth ministry leadership. Presumably, each parish or community will then be able to decide who should take on these roles, considering its staff, size, finances, and other factors.

The role of youth ministry program leader presented in this chapter is another example of that flexibility. The leadership for a given parish program may be held by an individual or a group, with or without a title. What is important is that someone in the parish give attention to sustaining and developing individual program efforts.

When is the role needed? As with the coordinator's role the answer to this question could also be "always." However, there are some instances in which it is more needed than others. For example, a youth minister trying to develop a comprehensive youth ministry in a large parish will only be able to do so if he or she also develops program leaders. This is because in a large parish it would not be possible to effectively provide leadership to the whole and all of the parts. On the other hand, a parish without a youth minister may have developed one or more programs for youth; it took leadership to begin the effort, and will take leadership to keep the program functioning well.

Who can or should fill the role? Program leaders may be youth or adults, may be volunteers or staff members, and may work individually or as a team. In the examples given so far, Denise, a DRE, was a program leader for the high school religious education program; and Irene and Dick, along with other team members, were program leaders for the in-home program. They all later became involved as coordinators of youth ministry, even while continuing with their previous task. (Leaders may fill *more* than one role!)

What is important is that these leaders have a sense of the whole — a realization of how this particular program fits in with other programs and with a comprehensive youth ministry. The understanding that no one person *is* youth ministry is essential for the leader.

What background or experience is needed? Leadership qualities and willingness are the keys. Needed knowledge and skills can be gained through training for the particular role. A coordinator of high school religious education will need different training than a coordinator of sports programs, but both need leadership training.

Pastoral Examples

The diversity of youth ministry leaders and programs that has evolved in recent years is one of the signs of the vitality of youth ministry. The reader will be able to add many examples to the few chosen here.

Trudy knew sign language because her brother was deaf. When she was fifteen she realized that the Liturgy of the Word was not proclaimed to the deaf. She asked that she be permitted to sign at Mass occasionally. Soon requests came from other parishes, so she organized a group of teenagers who were also willing to sign. Gradually they evolved a program so that every Sunday at one of the churches in their vicariate a liturgy was signed. In three short years Trudy found herself leading a program and giving workshops for others on the needs of the deaf and the role of youth in ministry. She had developed from being a minister to being a youth ministry program leader.

When Freda completed her M.A. in religious education she was hired by her parish to serve as coordinator of high school religious education. The part-time position was to her liking because she had children at home and because she used her skills and education. She involved many adults in teaching in the program by offering occasional minicourses and having guest lecturers. Freda provided both in-depth and crash-course training for the leaders, and involved many of them in working with her on the curriculum. She also planned occasional programs for the parents of the teens. While she recognized the need for a comprehensive youth ministry and advocated more programs to serve the needs of youth, she felt that neither time nor talent made it possible for her to develop them. Freda was a skilled and effective youth ministry program leader and an advocate for further youth ministry programs.

Bernie and Jim were enthusiastic mountain climbers. They liked teenagers and wanted to share their enthusiasm with them, so they began a mountaineering club. The climbs, the gab-fests along the way, and the celebration in prayer at the mountaintop provided many opportunities for ministry. They realized, however, that these events were too infrequent, so they began to involve other adults and some teen leaders in planning events for their club. Service projects, the production of a summer play, and various parties became part of the tradition. After ten years many former "mountaineers" came back to visit the group and to enjoy some of its events. Like Trudy, Bernie and Jim moved outward from their own ministry to planning with and enabling others.

Challenges

What difficulties arise when undertaking this task? Difficulties discussed in previous chapters often affect youth ministry program leaders too. The introduction of a possible new program is a change and may arouse resistance. It took time and patience for Freda to involve many lay adults in the religious education program, because in her parish it was traditional that the priests taught high school religion. The question of legitimacy sometimes is an issue. Bernie and Jim interacted with many priests and parents in the last ten years, some of whom challenged their right to be having a mountaineering club. They worked out the problem each time, but always concluded that their basic right to invite teens to go mountaineering rested with their membership in the community, and that a parent could always say no.

At times the leaders of individual programs fail to recognize that each program is (potentially, at least) only part of a larger whole. The "war" that sometimes goes on between the leaders of two programs is detrimental to youth ministry and to the life of the church.

Perhaps the most consistent difficulty is the pressure, from within the program or from the larger community, to make the individual program, and therefore its leaders, perform more of the task of youth ministry than they can. Freda, as religious education coordinator, was very clear about the fact that various needs of youth would best be met in another setting. That is why she advocated the development of a comprehensive youth ministry, with additional youth ministry program leaders.

How can these difficulties be met? Being able to name the nature of the problem is the first step in meeting some of the difficulties youth ministry program leaders encounter. Another important aid is increased understanding and skill in the leadership task. In the examples of Trudy and Bernie and Jim these leaders were first "doers." For the most part they learned how to plan, enable, and train by doing it; expanding their knowledge would help them understand their own successes and failures.

Reflection on the needs of youth and the way various programs can meet them would help give these leaders a better perspective on what they do. This would help them to recognize how their programs complement other programs. It would also give them a clearer understanding of what each program can and cannot do, so that neither internal nor external pressures would cause them to try to shape one program to do everything.

Summary

The activities and programs sponsored by a parish for its young people are the action arm of its total youth ministry. For many youth their primary contact with caring adults will be the result of participation in a program like sports, a drama group, or a faith-sharing group. Committed and skilled leadership of these opportunities for ministry is the task of the youth ministry program leader. Whether the program leader roles are assumed by the parish priests, a parent, or a teenage leader, these program leaders share a common responsibility to keep their specific program running smoothly and in cooperation with the other youth programs.

In summary there are three complementary leadership challenges for a parish that wishes to provide ministry to and with its youth. The role of the *youth ministry program leaders* is to sustain and develop the activities that are part of the parish youth ministry effort. The role of the *youth ministry team* is to plan, design and evaluate youth ministry activities in the parish. The role of the *youth ministry coordinator* is to harmonize the different people and programs that comprise the parish youth ministry and to provide vision and support for its growth.

Although one person often wears all three "hats" in a parish, the more people who can share in the leadership, the more vital and alive the youth ministry will be. The chapters in Part Three cover the specific skills that will help a parish recruit volunteers, conduct planning sessions, and train and support new leaders.

Part 3

Leadership in Action

The real test of leadership is in its actions. The chapters of Part Two clarified the roles and responsibilities of youth ministry leaders. This is important, but mostly because a good understanding of the job paves the way for effective action. In Part Three of this book the focus shifts to the practical functions of leadership that youth ministers are responsible for: planning, enablement, and training.

The planning function may be summarized by saying that the leader enables a group to know *why* they want to do something and *how* they will do it. The *why* is the crucial first step, in which the leader helps others to focus on their mission, their goal, and their purpose. This step is central to the planning process in any setting, but in ministry it has added importance because it is the point at which the group members ponder the meaning of their discipleship. The leader must help the group find and articulate its inspiration.

In determining the *how* of what will be done, all dimensions are included, from determining the needs to evaluating the results. Planning is a disciplined process which groups often want to short-circuit. However, a well-executed planning process is *itself* a part of ministry, even as it prepares a plan for further ministry. Attention to communication, development of accountability systems, conflict management, and ongoing education are additional parts of the planning task. Chapters 7 and 8 present the planning function in greater detail.

In keeping with the vision of the Church as the People of God and with an appreciation of the many gifts needed to develop a comprehensive youth ministry, a key task of the leader is calling forth the gifts of others and inviting them to ministry. This action is most effective when it proceeds in two ways. One way is from an observation of a need that exists in the parish, followed by a search for someone to meet that need. A second way is from observation of a gift that someone has, followed by a search for a way to use that gift. Generally church leaders have emphasized the first method, and it is needed. However, the second method is equally important and can lead to very creative and exciting forms of ministry.

When people are invited to share in ministry they have the right to receive the training and support they need in order to be effective. Chapters 9 and 10 take a thorough look at the specifics involved in enabling and training volunteers.

7
The Youth Minister As Planner

"American youth are all spiritually charged up, but they have no place to go."[1]

This statement was made by George Gallup, Jr., upon completing his research on "America's Faithful." In a very revealing report, Gallup produced figures showing that 71 percent of the surveyed youth said that their religious commitment is *the* most important or *one* of the most important influences in their lives. This figure has important implications for those who are working with youth within the Church. The figures vary in different settings, but many Catholic churches find that they are reaching less than 40 percent of their young people through present programs. If 71 percent are highly influenced yet less than 40 percent are involved, there is something wrong. Either there is nothing to get involved with in their parishes or what is offered is not what is desired.

The purpose of this chapter is to introduce a process for developing a comprehensive ministry to youth. The adolescent has been stereotyped as apathetic and disinterested. Gallup's research, as well as the experiences of scores of youth ministers, denies this stereotype and calls for quality programs. What the Church needs is a planned, well-informed approach to meeting the needs of young people.

Rationale for Planning

The word *planning* triggers an entire spectrum of thoughts and feelings in youth ministers. Some fear "too much structure," "no freedom," "lack of spontaneity," "long meetings." On the other hand, some cry, "Finally, organization!" "Now I know where to begin." "Now it's not just my job."

There are two different approaches to implementing a total youth ministry effort. Let us call the most common one the "Hunt-and-Peck Method": "We'll try this program or activity, and if it doesn't work we can try other ones until we get a good response." Attempt after attempt is made to find a program attractive enough to convince more youth to attend.

The second approach involves spending time on a systematic planning process. Some ministry leaders shy away from such a method; they don't want to be tied to a system or series of steps. (This is particularly true of those whose MBTI preference is perceiving.) However, the purpose of a planning process is to *free* the leader. The process suggested in the next chapter allows a total youth ministry to evolve with a predictability that provides time for creativity.

The rationale for this process is based on three principles:

First, when a person's needs are being met, he or she responds with continued involvement. The planning process begins with an assessment of the needs of the youth to be served. Programs are then developed to meet both individual and group concerns. This is known as the *needs-based* approach to planning. The contrasting method, programs based on *wants*, yields short-lived programs, because what someone wants may change quickly. Needs are more stationary. It should also be noted that programs based solely on tradition ("We've always done it that way.") may have no purpose or meaning for today's participants. Youth ministry leaders too often find themselves trying to sell youth on coming to an activity. If the activity is meeting the young person's perceived needs he or she will have personal motivation for attending, and a positive response is more likely.

The second principle says that when people feel *ownership* of an organization or a program, they will support it, defend it, and invite others to share in it. The primary purpose of a needs-based approach to planning is to create a shared ownership of the youth ministry. Youth ought to be consulted to determine the content of the program, and they should share in its implementation. When this happens young people feel that it is *their* program, *their* youth group, or *their* project. Otherwise it is someone else's idea or activity, which has nothing to do with them.

The way to build this sense of ownership is to follow a step-by-step plan that includes youth throughout the planning process. Youth ministers may be able to develop a fine program more quickly when they work on their own, but then they have to convince youth to attend. When young people do the planning with the youth minister their attendance is much more likely.

The third principle states that good communication is vital for effective ministry. There are many organizations which attempt to attract the attention of teenagers, and many people either affect or are affected by what teenagers do. In order for the Church to reach into the lives of young people in a meaningful way, shared ownership of the youth ministry effort must extend beyond the youth themselves. Parents, school personnel, and community officials must also be communicated with and be a part of the Church's effort. This will open up all kinds of channels and create a broad base of support for the leaders' efforts. The planning process offers a structured opportunity to make these contacts.

An Overview of the Planning Process

Planning a total youth ministry program takes the long-range efforts of a number of people. Planning is one of the key tasks that can appropriately be done by a youth ministry team. (See chapter 5.) Their job will demand cooperation and collaboration as they work together to clarify their vision of youth ministry.

It is important that the team as a whole start the process with a clear understanding of the steps involved and the time that it will take.

Although the planning team need not be made up of the same people who will be responsible for implementing the final plan, normally some members of the team are program leaders also. The actual composition of a planning team will vary according to the unique parish situation, but the importance of diversity in experience and representation remains the same. The following list summarizes the guidelines described in chapter 5 for the formation of a team.

- SIZE—ten to fifteen people.
- AGE—about half youth and half adult.
- REPRESENTATION—parish priest if possible, some informed and interested parents, a young adult already out of high school, representatives of adults already involved in youth programs, the person responsible for high school religious education, youth representatives of the different high school age groups.

The planning process itself involves eight steps, which are outlined on the next page and explained in the next chapter.

Usually a time period of about three months is necessary to complete steps one through six before implementing new programs. Steps two and six require the most time. If the team starts in the late spring the new plans may be ready to carry out by the start of the fall season.

Youth Ministry Program Planning Process Chart

PLANNING STEP 1: Taking stock	**PLANNING STEP 2:** Assessing needs	**PLANNING STEP 3:** Analyzing data	**PLANNING STEP 4:** Developing mission and objectives
TASKS a. Evaluate past and present programming in terms of *Vision of Youth Ministry*. b. Gather feedback from those affected by present programs, adults and youth.	TASKS a. Examine choice of data-gathering tools. b. Carry out the needs assessment using appropriate tools and methods.	TASKS a. Tally gathered data. b. Prioritize needs.	TASKS a. Write a mission statement. b. Write objectives for youth ministry.
PLANNING STEP 5: Designing programs	**PLANNING STEP 6:** Developing a leadership system	**PLANNING STEP 7:** Implementing programs	**PLANNING STEP 8:** Evaluating youth ministry
TASKS a. Brainstorm activities to meet objectives. b. Choose appropriate activities for each objective. c. Write plan of action for each activity.	TASKS a. Develop an organizational system. b. Enlist, train, and supervise volunteers.	TASKS Prepare and monitor calendar and general program management.	TASKS a. Develop tool(s). b. Implement review.

Youth Ministry Program
Planning Process

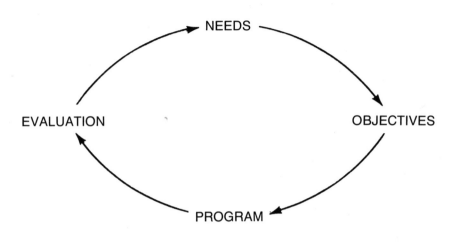

Notes

1. From George Gallup, Jr., and David Poling, *The Search for America's Faith* (Nashville: Abingdon Press, 1980).

8
Eight Steps to Program Planning

This chapter describes each step of the program planning process along with the resources and worksheets that accompany them.

STEP 1: Taking Stock

At the end of a youth ministry planning workshop with parish volunteers, it is fairly common for someone to comment, "You know, I didn't realize that we were doing as much as we are for the youth in our parish." Because concerned parents and leaders want to see improvements in a parish youth ministry, they have a tendency to underestimate the potential in the ways that the parish currently touches the lives of youth.

This first step in the planning process, then, is designed to give the planning team an opportunity to assess the present state of youth ministry in the parish. This review can give the team a valuable perspective and a common starting point. It acknowledges what is being done now and what has taken place through the efforts of others. It also fosters a readiness for an expansion of the vision of youth ministry in the parish.

Since many people have the inclination to see youth ministry in program terms only, it is important that this assessment be done with the components of youth ministry as they are outlined in *A Vision of Youth Ministry.* As the team begins to identify, for example, the ways in which youth participate in worship or service projects or community celebrations, it can gain insight into the great diversity of ways that youth can be involved—many of them far easier to initiate than people might imagine.

This first step can be done very thoroughly or in a more general fashion, depending upon how active the parish has been with respect to youth ministry opportunities. Worksheet 1 at the end of the chapter will provide a general review for parishes that have not had a great deal of youth programming. To use this worksheet, the planning team should first read or discuss the goals and components of youth ministry. (See chapter 1 for a summary.) Then the leader of the group should facilitate a group brainstorming session in which members of the team identify the ways in which the parish currently fulfills the intention of each component. For example, under "worship" they might list the teen folk group, youth lectors, and an annual youth Mass. After the group has named all of the ways in which the parish ministers to or with youth, each overall component should be evaluated on a scale of 1 (little or nothing offered) to 5 (effective programs offered).

The resources in Step 2, "assessing needs," provide an alternative way to take stock of the youth ministry situation, especially for parishes with a pre-existing youth program of some kind. Worksheet 2 is a survey that each member of the planning team can fill out. It identifies the relative importance of different goals and assesses the effectiveness with which the parish is currently achieving them.

The process of listing, evaluating, and discussing present youth ministry efforts in the parish should result in a clearer sense of the starting point for members of the team. It will also help to build a common philosophy and direction, which will become critical at the point of creating goals and objectives.

STEP 2: Assessing Needs

Chapter 7 made it clear that youth ministry programs built on real needs are more enduring than programs that respond to "wants." This is a delicate distinction to make, because young people and adults do not always see eye-to-eye on the needs or wants of youth. At this stage of the planning process the team should collect as much information as possible about the youth of the community—their situations, their backgrounds, beliefs, attitudes, involvements, and interests. The information that is gathered should come from young people, obviously, but also from their parents, concerned parishioners, and local community leaders. The more sources of data that can be tapped, the broader the perspective of the team on the needs of youth.

A comment on the process is in order at this point: Gathering information, in one sense, is a simple task that must be organized and then carried out more or less efficiently. However, asking people questions is also an active form of ministry. It involves people, their thinking is shaped by the questions they are asked, and their sense of ownership in the final product is heightened. Therefore it is important that the planning team members use sensitivity when they carry out the data-gathering step. Surveys and interviews should be conducted with the same friendliness, attentiveness, concern, and respect that would be expected of the youth ministry program when it is in operation.

A variety of methods can be chosen by the team to assess the needs of youth. Parents, neighbors, and young people know a lot about the needs of youth from their own observations. A representative planning team will jointly have many observations to contribute. These ideas can be recorded on large sheets of newsprint during a general meeting of the planning team.

The results of the youth ministry assessment that was done at Step 1 can provide some insights into current needs also. Established members of the parish might be tapped to discover an *historical perspective* on the needs of youth in the parish. This is a good way to acknowledge the hard work of earlier youth ministry leaders, and also enables the team to avoid repeating past mistakes.

Interviews are a very valuable way to gather data and also to open lines of communication with key teenagers and with important adults. The planning team can build connections in the community and increase ownership in the youth ministry effort by talking to all those who interact with youth, such as teachers, town leaders, parks and recreation staff, the police, civic organization leaders, neighboring parishes, youth group leaders of other denominations, youth employers, store owners, and teen members of various school and community groups.

If the planning team decides to interview people, the interviews should be assigned to team members who are most comfortable with the different interviewees. A convenient time for the interview should be set that will allow the planning team member enough time to introduce himself or herself and to explain the nature and purpose of the youth ministry planning process. Notes should be kept of the comments made by the interviewees, and they should be contacted later by mail or in person to thank them for their help.

Written instruments such as surveys, evaluation forms, and reaction sheets are perhaps the most commonly used ways of gathering information from a large number of people. A written instrument has the advantage of allowing people to express themselves as fully as they choose, but the drawback is that surveys can be hard to collect once they are sent out. Distributing them in person at parish functions tends to guarantee a better rate of return, but it also means that uninvolved adults or youth are not represented in the responding group. A combination of mailing surveys and giving some in person is probably the best way to ensure a wide response.

Worksheet 2 is a comprehensive survey in two parts, one for adults and one for youth. They are compatible instruments which attempt to gather data on the success with which the parish is meeting various needs of youth. (Note that the cover page with directions should be included whether the survey is going to an adult or to a youth.)

Worksheet 3 is a sample parent survey that is simpler in form and focused on gathering information from the parents of the teenagers. Worksheet 4 is a general interview form that can be used with community leaders. Each of these resources can be modified according to the preferences of the planning team.

A sample of a Youth Sunday talk is at the end of this chapter. Some parishes have combined the tasks of educating the parish to youth ministry and doing a needs assessment of adults and youth. A special Youth Ministry Sunday is a way to accomplish such a task. Teenage youth may help plan the Sunday liturgy; assist as ushers, lectors, and other liturgical ministers; speak at Masses;

and host a reception afterward. Surveys could be distributed either during the Mass or at the reception.

When the surveys, interviews, and discussions have been completed and the information is written and collected, the team is ready to move on to the next step, analyzing the data.

STEP 3: Analyzing Data

If the planning team has done a good job of gathering information about young people in the community, it will be natural for them to feel a bit overwhelmed when they begin to analyze this data. However, the analysis is the key that transforms a collection of facts and opinions into a meaningful guide for future action. The analysis step lets the team sort out what it has learned, see the overall patterns, and name the priorities to which it will respond.

The first thing the team must do is collate the responses to the questions it has asked in person or on questionnaires. (Worksheet 2-C is a tally sheet that can be used to summarize the responses to the youth and adult surveys in Worksheets 2-A and 2-B.) Collating involves grouping together all of the different answers that were given for similar questions. For example, a single list could be made that names the needs of youth from the point of view of parents, then this list should be placed side by side with the list of youth needs as they are perceived by community leaders and by young people.

Since the entire team should agree on the analysis of the data, a good way to easily review all of the information is to have the data posted in summary fashion on newsprint sheets. As the team looks over the lists, their next task is to group the data into major categories. Perhaps the responses from several different sources seem to agree on the lack of any community place for teenagers to meet. Or the interviews may have uncovered a widespread concern about family conflicts or alcohol abuse among teens.

The interviews may also have alerted the team to available resources, such as a community-based service for alcohol and drug abuse counseling, or an interdenominational program on parent-teen communication. Perhaps the team has discovered how many youth belong to the parish, what schools they attend, and how many are involved in the parish programs.

Information like this could be usefully grouped under categories such as "Needs," "Resources," and "General Information," as in the examples below:

Needs:

1) Parents and teens are having trouble communicating.
2) There is no place for youth to gather in the community.
3) The parish has no program for the spiritual growth of older adolescents.
4) The problem of alcohol abuse is growing among teens.

Resources available:

1) The community library has an excellent selection of films for youth.
2) The parish has a good group of adults who are willing to volunteer their time.
3) The community has a drug abuse resource center.

General information:

1) There are 350 teenagers registered in the parish.
2) Two-thirds of the youth attend public schools, one-third are in Catholic schools.
3) Fifty young people are regularly touched by current parish programs.

Since the list of "needs" will be used as a guide for planning, the team should work carefully on this list, clustering related items to see if they point to a more basic common need. When the list seems complete the team will finish the process of analyzing the data by discussing the relative priority of each need.

The priority discussion is *not* an attempt to say that one need is more important than another; rather, it is a way of identifying both the needs that are pressing *and* the needs that the youth ministry planning team can realistically address in the coming year. High priority should go to needs that are of broad concern and that can be helped by the response of the parish. Priorities can be listed in order: 1, 2, 3, etc., or they can be grouped first into A, B, C categories and then numbered.

All the members of the planning group and the key leaders (such as the pastor) should agree on the analysis of the collected data. Unless they come to some degree of consensus at this point, the subsequent program will not receive full support. It is worthwhile spending time to reach agreement on the analysis, because a common motivation eliminates many of the obstacles that a team can face in planning and carrying out programs.

STEP 4: Developing Mission and Objectives

Although most pastoral planning processes *begin* with the development of a mission statement, experience indicates that a newly formed youth ministry planning team handles this step better later on in the planning process. There are two reasons for this: To begin with, the team actually has an implicit mission by the very fact that it has been formed and charged with the job of planning. Furthermore, the task of writing that mission in ways that are agreeable to the whole group can be a frustrating exercise for the members, who more than likely are highly motivated to begin identifying and meeting the needs of young people. So, although the mission can appropriately be written as the first step, it appears in this process as Step 4 along with the objectives.

There is often confusion between mission, goals, objectives, strategies, and the many other words that are used in planning. Each system of planning may define these concepts slightly differently, but the principle remains the same; namely, the ultimate results that the team is planning for should be spelled out broadly at first, then more specifically, and then with concrete, measurable detail.

In this planning process, mission and objectives are defined as follows:

Mission Statement: A mission is a statement of purpose for youth ministry in the parish. It should provide broad direction without mentioning particular hopes. It may serve as a uniting factor for the planning team, as it summarizes the ultimate end that the team's efforts are building toward. A mission statement is characteristically short and simple, stating general functions and directions. It is timeless; it names basic commitments and who is to be served.

Objectives: Objectives are statements of what the youth ministry program plans to accomplish within a given period of time, such as three years or one year. They name concrete, measurable results. They can be designed as a direct response to a priority need, and they can also be written to accomplish any of the seven components of youth ministry. (See chapter 1.) Objectives should start with the word "to" and be followed with an action verb. Objectives should be written realistically, in such a way that it will be possible later to measure whether or not the objective was successfully achieved. Objectives should leave the listener with the question, "But how?" (The "how" question is answered in the next step of the process, when the team creates programs and activities that will fulfill the objectives.)

It is often awkward for a group any larger than three to work on the same statement. The process that works best for the writing of a mission statement is for the planning team to discuss its mission, list on newsprint the key points that people have made, agree on the basic idea, then delegate the task of drafting a statement to one of the team members. (This is a good way to use the talents of those who write well, especially if they are quieter members of the group.) The group can discuss the first draft produced by the writer, then revise it if necessary, or discuss it further and ask for a second draft. When a statement is written that incorporates the thinking of the group and the intention of the parish, and when all members of the team can agree with what it says, the statement becomes the mission of the youth ministry.

Objectives can be created in a different manner. First, the team should decide on the time frame for the objectives: Will they be one year in duration? two years? three years? Newer efforts will do best with short-range objectives, although the long-range picture is eventually very important for healthy development of the ministry.

Since the intent of each objective may end up being fulfilled by three or five or more different activities or programs, it is wise to limit the number of objectives to a reasonable number. Seven or eight should be sufficient to encompass the aims of even a very lively youth ministry program.

Two different methods can be used to create a list of objectives. As the example below indicates, objectives can be written as a response to the top priority needs that the team generated so far in the planning process. A second method is to create objectives that correspond to the components of youth ministry. (A sample of such objectives can be found in Worksheet 1.)

Objectives based on needs

Need: Teenagers like to help people. *Objective:* To develop youth service programs to help our community.

Need: Teenagers want to learn more about their religion. *Objective:* To provide spiritual programs for the youth of our parish to assist them in integrating religious values into their everyday lives.

Need: Youth need to have fun with their friends. *Objective:* To provide social programs for the youth of our parish.

Need: Teenagers need to talk to sympathetic helpers about personal problems. *Objective:* To provide youth with guidance in the areas of personal, social, and family problems.

The time spent in gathering and analyzing information about the needs of youth pays off at this step of the planning process because the needs assessment and the mission together give the team a good sense of direction. Creativity begins to run free. In fact, the most common problem groups have in writing objectives is that the tendency to get to the solution pushes them too quickly past objectives and into programs or activities. The planning team should resist this by evaluating their list of objectives according to the criteria that are given in the definition. (If a lot of good answers to the "But how?" question keep popping up while the group is working on objectives, it is a good idea to keep a running record of these ideas on a separate sheet of newsprint so that they will not be lost. The team will be well ahead of the game when it comes to Step 5!)

STEP 5: Designing Programs

The first four steps of the planning process lay the foundation and build the frame for a coordinated youth ministry program in a parish. At the fifth step, the team begins the far more detailed process of choosing and designing the actual activities, events, and programs that will be offered in the parish over the next six months or year.

Designing should begin by stimulating creativity through a brainstorming process. Then the ideas that have been generated can be critiqued, refined, and mapped out as concrete plans.

The team should take each objective, one at a time, and ask the question, "What activities or opportunities can we offer to meet this objective?" With someone assigned to write ideas onto a sheet of newsprint or blackboard, the group can begin to brainstorm any and all possible answers to the question. (The rules of brainstorming say that anyone's idea, no matter how farfetched it may seem, should be written down without criticism from another group member. The chance to rule out impractical ideas comes later.)

For example:

Objective: To provide social and recreational opportunities to build community among the youth of the parish.

Ideas:

Dances	Christmas carolling
Gym nights	Ski trip
Summer picnic	Movie outings
Send teens to diocesan convention	Pizza-making party
Summer softball	

Objective: To offer programs for catechesis and spiritual formation for young people of high-school age.

Ideas:

Fall and spring overnight retreats
SHARING group
Holy Week programs of liturgy, scriptural study, and service to the needy
Series of six-week minicourses on Church, Jesus, relationships, moral choices, etc.
Offer spiritual direction
Sunday evening speaker series
Set up a library shelf for spiritual reading suitable for teens
Religious awards programs for Scouting and Campfire organizations

When the brainstorming process has been done for each objective, the team should have a sizeable list of possible activities to choose from. Obviously, what the group must do next is select from that list the activities that seem best. This is simple to say, but can be difficult to do. Some ideas need to be researched a bit before they can be endorsed. For example, if someone suggests starting a "gym night" to provide a recreational program for the teens, it may be necessary to check with the parish staff first to discover the availability of the gym and to lobby on behalf of the teens to win permission to use it!

Other ideas that might need advance research would be out-of-town trips, interdenominational projects, and similar activities that involve expenses or resources that are beyond the immediate control of the parish. If several of the most promising ideas need some advance researching, the team might assign individuals or small committees to gather the necesssary information and then report back to the team for a decision-making session.

The programs and activities that are selected by the team for the youth ministry calendar should meet several criteria. The questions below are examples of the criteria that can be used.

1) Is the program consistent with our mission and our understanding of youth ministry?
2) Will this program be acceptable to the youth and adults of our community, considering our traditions and values?
3) Is the timing right for this program? (Are we ready for it yet? Does it conflict with something important?)
4) Do we have the resources that we need (money, time, people, materials) to do this program successfully?
5) Does this program duplicate services that are already done well by schools, agencies, or other churches? If so, is duplication wise?
6) Are different kinds of youth being reached by the various programs that have been selected?

The next part of the designing process involves writing up a plan of action for each activity or program that the team chooses to do. The plan should include dates and times, location, how many leaders and helpers will be needed, necessary materials or funds, and an outline of the tasks that have to be accomplished to carry out and evaluate the program. Worksheet 5 is a sample planning activity sheet that can be filled out for each program. Since the step requires some detail work, it is best to delegate the work to individuals and small committees, or two or three people.

In fact, if the program needs leaders that must be recruited, the actual time and place and procedure details, in some cases, can be left blank for the newly recruited leaders to plan. Then the whole team can review, refine, and adopt the final plans. It is especially important that the team mark all of the planned events on a master calendar, so that they can detect any possible conflicts or overly busy months.

A word of caution: The team might be most successful if it plans a relatively small number of programs that are done well, rather than a flurry of events that are poorly coordinated or done without proper preparation, leadership, or materials.

STEP 6: Developing a Leadership System

In the planning process, the volunteers that are needed for the youth ministry program are enlisted after the events are selected and designed. This method has the advantage of allowing the recruiters to ask volunteers if they would be willing to do very specific tasks, with time commitments and duties spelled out. The recruitment, training, and support of volunteers is a crucial part of the leadership task of youth ministry. The chapters which follow give a detailed overview of the process of enabling volunteers. The work of this step may be done by the planning team itself, by the coordinator, or by a smaller task force of the team. For the youth ministry coordinator, whether he or she is paid or a volunteer, there is no more important single aspect of the job than to learn how to organize other people to help in the work. To attempt the job solo is a recipe for early burnout; to successfully use the talents of volunteers is to share the ministry in growthful and creative ways.

STEP 7: Implementing the Program

At this point, the role of the leadership team or of the coordinator is good management of the programs that the team has planned. The management tasks include keeping lines of communication open, setting up a good publicity system for the program, watching the budget and scheduling fund-raising projects, and keeping the calendar up-to-date. When publicizing the program, it helps to remind parishioners of their input during the needs assessment phase, pointing out that the program has been created in response to their ideas.

Over the months, different volunteers might share these tasks by taking on responsibility for a telephone chain to let the teens know about upcoming events, or forming committees to do bulletin announcements, posters, and other forms of publicity. Usually, the funding of the program is worked out in close consultation with the parish staff at the beginning of the fiscal year.

STEP 8: Evaluating Youth Ministry

Evaluation is the last step in any planning process, and unfortunately it is too often neglected. Evaluation is the activity that "closes the loop," bringing the leaders in touch once more with present needs and new possibilities for meeting those needs. Evaluation feeds directly into the next cycle of planning.

Three different opportunities for evaluation can be helpful to the leaders of youth ministry programs:

The first type of evaluation is the review that can be scheduled after each major event or activity. This evaluation is intended to discover how the participants felt about the program, what they learned or enjoyed most, how well organized the event was, what could have been done better, and, overall, whether or not it fulfilled its purpose.

A second type of evaluation is the midyear check-in. This can be a survey or discussion halfway through the program season that gives adult and teen leaders a chance to review how things are going. Besides giving the leaders a chance to make any mid-course corrections that seem necessary, the evaluation discussion can also provide a boost of commitment and motivation, since it involves a new look at the mission and objectives of the team and its success in meeting them.

The third level of evaluation is the thorough review that should come at the end of the program year or season. Through interviews, observations, or surveys the team is able to gather data from volunteers, parish staff, parents, teens, and others. The data should indicate whether the team successfully reached its objectives. It might also point to new needs that can become the basis for the next planning cycle. A sample program evaluation method is found in Worksheet 6.

RESOURCE: Youth Sunday Talk

Good morning, I'm _____ . Today, on Youth Sunday, I would like to take this opportunity to explain the Parish Youth Ministry to you. At this time, we will share our knowledge, and it is hoped you will share your feelings concerning this proposed program.

What is youth ministry? Youth ministry is the response of the Christian community to the needs of our young people, and the sharing of the unique gifts of youth with the whole community. By answering the needs of youth, the community in turn receives a wealth of gifts that can *only* be given by *youth*. Even though _____ youth have many neglected needs, they also have an abundance of resources to offer to their community. The giving and receiving between youth and community is youth ministry.

Youth ministry has several basic goals. First, it tries to develop the total person. Youth ministry is concerned with every aspect of young people's lives. It aims to foster and support the growth of each individual. Youth ministry also seeks to encourage young people to accept responsibility in life and in their community. Through studies, workshops, and learning adventures youth will gain a knowledge of their responsibilities. This goal is certainly needed here in _____ where some teenagers feel alienated from church and community.

Even though youth ministry is to youth, with youth, by youth, and for youth, non-youth also play a role in this program. Since all adults were once teenagers, their experience and knowledge is very valuable. Although youth leadership is stressed, adults will take part in the program as advisors and organizers. Although we sometimes deny it, we need adults in our youth ministry.

Youth ministry is the attempt to satisfy youth's spiritual and social needs. It can accomplish these goals through learning experiences, workshops, and social events.

A youth ministry effort is now being set up here in _____ _____ . An organizing committee has had _____ meetings since _____ . The group is nearing the completion of its first objective, which is to obtain information from many members of the parish — teenagers and adults — concerning what they would like in the program. This information will enable the group to design a program that is acceptable to the parish. The planning group is now receiving data through different methods. Members of that group are interviewing leaders in our community such as our mayor, other ministers, police officers, and school administrators. These interviews consist of asking questions dealing with our youth and possible programs. We also have the results of a poll given to _____ high school students that surveyed their desired social activities. Today, as part of Youth Sunday, the final survey will be given. _____ will conduct it now.

Since we want to base this program on your ideas, we ask you to fill out the survey. Because we are a parish family and the youth program is of interest to all of us, we really need your ideas.

We have prepared two surveys, one for high schoolers, and one for parents and interested adults. _____ and _____ _____ are handing out _____ sheets to high schoolers and _____ sheets to the adults.

Since we cannot speak to you personally, as we would like, we ask you to be as candid as possible with your answers.

When you are finished, please hold on to your survey and the helpers will come around and collect them.

If there are any questions, we will be happy to answer them after Mass. Thank you for your cooperation; the results will be printed in a future bulletin.

WORKSHEET 1: Taking Stock of Youth Ministry

Directions: On this worksheet, list the programs, activities, or opportunities that are *currently* available to youth in each of the seven components of youth ministry. Then evaluate the degree to which each component is successfully addressed. On the scale, 1 is low (little or nothing offered in this area) and 5 is high (effective programs and services offered).

1. **Word**

To guide young persons' growth in faith and spirituality through formal and informal catechesis, and to identify and reach out to young people who are outside the church community with the witness of the gospel message (evangelization).

Current Responses:

Evaluation:

1   2   3   4   5

2. **Worship**

To promote liturgies and prayer experiences for young people to share the questions, joys, and struggles of their lives with other youth, their families, and adults in the context of the Christian community.

Current Responses:

Evaluation:

1   2   3   4   5

3. **Creating Community**

To provide opportunities for young people to share the questions, joys, and struggles of their lives with other youth, their families, and adults in the context of the Christian community.

Current Responses:

Evaluation:

1   2   3   4   5

4. **Justice and Service** To witness the Church's active concern for those who suffer from poverty, handicaps, and injustice, and to sponsor programs for youth that involve service, reflection, and education for justice.

Current Responses:

Evaluation:

1   2   3   4   5

5. **Guidance and Healing** To provide youth with sources of support and counsel as they face personal, spiritual, and vocational decisions, and to foster healing and reconciliation in their lives and relationships.

Current Responses:

Evaluation:

1   2   3   4   5

6. **Enablement** To develop, support, and utilize the leadership abilities and personal gifts of youth and adults, encouraging their active participation in the responsibilities of ministry to other youth and adults.

Current Responses:

Evaluation:

1   2   3   4   5

7. **Advocacy** To interpret the needs of youth and to advocate their concerns to the Church and community.

Current Responses:

Evaluation:

1   2   3   4   5

WORSHEET 2A: Shared Vision of Youth Ministry

Directions: Your responses to the survey on the following pages will provide information that can help us develop a plan for our youth ministry. The survey lists youth ministry goals that a parish may have. For each goal statement you are asked to give *two* responses:

Importance

Toward what goals should our parish youth ministry be working

To the *left* of each goal statement, indicate how important you think that goal *should be* for the parish.

Circle one of six numbers:

6 = Extremely important
5 = Very important
4 = Important
3 = Somewhat important
2 = Slightly important
1 = Unimportant

Achievement

How well are we achieving these goals?

To the *right* of each goal statement, indicate with what success that goal is *actually being achieved* by the parish.

Circle one of seven numbers:

6 = Excellent
5 = Very good
4 = Good
3 = Adequate
2 = Only fair/Not so good
1 = Poor
NA = Not applicable

- Read the entire survey first.
- Speak for yourself; give your honest opinion.
- Vary your responses. You might begin filling out the survey thinking all of the goals are extremely important, but some goals are more important than others, and every parish does some things better than others. Show these variations in your responses.

_____ Pastor   _____ Youth minister _____ Parent

_____ Associate pastor   _____ Pastoral   _____ Concerned
                                  minister   parishioner

_____ Director of   _____ Adult   _____ Youth member
       religious   volunteer   of the parish
       education

Parish: _____

WORKSHEET 2B: Adult Survey Goals for Youth Ministry

In light of the needs of youth in our parish, how important are these goals?
(EXTREMELY IMPORTANT 6, VERY IMPORTANT 5, IMPORTANT 4, SOMEWHAT IMPORTANT 3, SLIGHTLY IMPORTANT 2, UNIMPORTANT 1)

In your view, with what success is this goal being achieved by our youth ministry?
(EXCELLENT 6, VERY GOOD 5, GOOD 4, ADEQUATE 3, ONLY FAIR, NOT SO GOOD 2, POOR 1, NOT APPLICABLE NA)

Goal	Importance	Success
1. To create a climate where young people can share their struggles, questions, and joys with other youth and adults.	6 5 4 3 2 1	6 5 4 3 2 1 NA
2. To help young people feel like a valued part of the parish and to encourage their participation in every aspect of parish life.	6 5 4 3 2 1	6 5 4 3 2 1 NA
3. To provide social and recreational activities where youth can build relationships.	6 5 4 3 2 1	6 5 4 3 2 1 NA
4. To identify and reach out to young people who are not active in the church community.	6 5 4 3 2 1	6 5 4 3 2 1 NA
5. To invite young people to experience a personal relationship with Jesus Christ.	6 5 4 3 2 1	6 5 4 3 2 1 NA
6. To guide the development of faith and Christian values in young people.	6 5 4 3 2 1	6 5 4 3 2 1 NA

Performance scale (top): EXCELLENT 6 | VERY GOOD 5 | GOOD 4 | ADEQUATE 3 | ONLY FAIR, NOT SO GOOD 2 | POOR 1 | NOT APPLICABLE NA

Item	Performance	Importance
7. To assist young people in developing a healthy self-concept about one's value and worthiness as a person.	6 5 4 3 2 1 NA	6 5 4 3 2 1
8. To assist young people in understanding the Scriptures and their meaning for one's life.	6 5 4 3 2 1 NA	6 5 4 3 2 1
9. To enable young people to make moral decisions based upon Christian values.	6 5 4 3 2 1 NA	6 5 4 3 2 1
10. To assist young people in acquiring a knowledge of human sexuality and to form a responsible Christian approach in sexual matters.	6 5 4 3 2 1 NA	6 5 4 3 2 1
11. To assist young people in developing an appreciation for what is unique about the Catholic faith.	6 5 4 3 2 1 NA	6 5 4 3 2 1
12. To assist young people in developing an understanding of the history of the Catholic Church.	6 5 4 3 2 1 NA	6 5 4 3 2 1
13. To foster the spiritual growth of young people through liturgies and prayer experiences.	6 5 4 3 2 1 NA	6 5 4 3 2 1
14. To help young people develop a personal prayer life.	6 5 4 3 2 1 NA	6 5 4 3 2 1

Importance scale (bottom): EXTREMELY IMPORTANT 6 | VERY IMPORTANT 5 | IMPORTANT 4 | SOMEWHAT IMPORTANT 3 | SLIGHTLY IMPORTANT 2 | UNIMPORTANT 1

15. To understand the place of the sacraments in the Christian life and to appreciate the importance of participating in the sacraments (especially the Eucharist and penance).
6 5 4 3 2 1 NA

16. To encourage the participation of young people in the liturgical life and ministries of the parish community.
6 5 4 3 2 1 NA

17. To strengthen the family life of youth.
6 5 4 3 2 1 NA

18. To provide youth with sources of support and counsel as they face personal, spiritual, and vocational decisions.
6 5 4 3 2 1 NA

19. To foster healing and reconciliation in young people's lives and relationships.
6 5 4 3 2 1 NA

20. To help young people experience God's grace and forgiveness (especially through the Sacrament of Reconciliation).
6 5 4 3 2 1 NA

21. To provide appropriate support and guidance for youth during times of stress and crisis.
6 5 4 3 2 1 NA

22. To respond to youth who suffer from poverty, handicaps, and injustice.
6 5 4 3 2 1 NA

23. To understand the Church's teachings on social justice and the Christian's responsibility for combating injustices.
6 5 4 3 2 1 NA

24. To involve young people in reaching out to serve people in need in their community and world.
6 5 4 3 2 1 NA

25. To develop, support, and utilize the leadership abilities and personal gifts of adults, encouraging their active participation in ministry to youth.
6 5 4 3 2 1 NA

26. To develop, support, and utilize the leadership abilities and personal gifts of youth, encouraging their active participation in ministry to other youth and adults.

6 5 4 3 2 1 NA

27. To provide for the ongoing development of youth ministry by establishing a leadership team of youth and adults who plan and coordinate the various aspects of youth ministry.

6 5 4 3 2 1 NA

28. To develop collaborative projects between our youth ministry and those of other churches (Protestant and Catholic) in your area.

6 5 4 3 2 1 NA

29. To interpret the needs of youth and to advocate their concerns to leaders in the church and community.

6 5 4 3 2 1 NA

30. To provide for the ongoing education of the parish community to the needs of youth and the purpose and direction of the youth ministry.

6 5 4 3 2 1 NA

Please list the goals above that you consider to be your top priority.

WORKSHEET 2C: Youth Survey Goals for Youth Ministry

In light of the needs of youth in our parish, how important are these goals?

6 = EXTREMELY IMPORTANT · 5 = VERY IMPORTANT · 4 = IMPORTANT · 3 = SOMEWHAT IMPORTANT · 2 = SLIGHTLY IMPORTANT · 1 = UNIMPORTANT

In your view, with what success is this goal being achieved by our youth ministry?

6 = EXCELLENT · 5 = VERY GOOD · 4 = GOOD · 3 = ADEQUATE · 2 = ONLY FAIR, NOT SO GOOD · 1 = POOR · NA = NOT APPLICABLE

I would like my parish to provide me with the opportunities to:

Importance	Goal	Success
6 5 4 3 2 1	1. Share my struggles, questions, and joys with others who accept me in an accepting community.	6 5 4 3 2 1 NA
6 5 4 3 2 1	2. Feel a part of the parish and participate in parish activities.	6 5 4 3 2 1 NA
6 5 4 3 2 1	3. Participate in recreational and social activities.	6 5 4 3 2 1 NA
6 5 4 3 2 1	4. Develop a closer relationship with Jesus.	6 5 4 3 2 1 NA
6 5 4 3 2 1	5. Meet with other youth and develop friendships.	6 5 4 3 2 1 NA
6 5 4 3 2 1	6. Develop an understanding of the Scriptures and their meaning for my life.	6 5 4 3 2 1 NA
6 5 4 3 2 1	7. Learn how to make moral decisions.	6 5 4 3 2 1 NA
6 5 4 3 2 1	8. Learn about the Christian view of sex, dating, and marriage.	6 5 4 3 2 1 NA
6 5 4 3 2 1	9. Learn what it means to be a Catholic today.	6 5 4 3 2 1 NA
6 5 4 3 2 1	10. Learn the history of the Catholic Church.	6 5 4 3 2 1 NA

						Item							
6	5	4	3	2	1	11. Understand the sacraments and what they mean for my life.	6	5	4	3	2	1	NA
6	5	4	3	2	1	12. Participate in liturgies and prayer experiences.	6	5	4	3	2	1	NA
6	5	4	3	2	1	13. Learn how to pray.	6	5	4	3	2	1	NA
6	5	4	3	2	1	14. Participate in the liturgical life of the parish as a lector, song leader, usher, etc.	6	5	4	3	2	1	NA
6	5	4	3	2	1	15. Learn how to improve communication with parents.	6	5	4	3	2	1	NA
6	5	4	3	2	1	16. Learn how to make decisions about career and college plans.	6	5	4	3	2	1	NA
6	5	4	3	2	1	17. Talk problems through with trusted adults.	6	5	4	3	2	1	NA
6	5	4	3	2	1	18. Learn how to cope with personal problems.	6	5	4	3	2	1	NA
6	5	4	3	2	1	19. Become more aware of people who suffer from poverty, handicaps, and injustice.	6	5	4	3	2	1	NA
6	5	4	3	2	1	20. Understand the Church's teachings on social justice and the Christian response.	6	5	4	3	2	1	NA
6	5	4	3	2	1	21. Be of service to the people in my community or neighborhood.	6	5	4	3	2	1	NA
6	5	4	3	2	1	22. Assume leadership.	6	5	4	3	2	1	NA

Comments:

WORKSHEET 2D: Tally Sheet for Shared Vision Survey
(Worksheets 2B and 2C)

Instructions: Using the appropriate column, place the average score in the correct item number. When developing goals, use the adult worksheet as a guide.

In light of the needs of youth in our parish, how important are these goals?

AVERAGE OF ADULT WORKSHEET	AVERAGE OF YOUTH WORKSHEET	COMBINED AVERAGE
1. ____	1. ____	1. ____
2. ____	2. ____	2. ____
3. ____	3. ____	3. ____
4. ____	5. ____	4. ____
5. ____	4. ____	5. ____
6. ____		6. ____
7. ____		7. ____
8. ____	6. ____	8. ____
9. ____	7. ____	9. ____
10. ____	8. ____	10. ____
11. ____	9. ____	11. ____
12. ____	10. ____	12. ____
13. ____	12. ____	13. ____
14. ____	13. ____	14. ____
15. ____	11. ____	15. ____
16. ____	14. ____	16. ____
17. ____	15. ____	17. ____
18. ____	16. ____	18. ____
19. ____	17. ____	19. ____
20. ____		20. ____
21. ____	18. ____	21. ____
22. ____	19. ____	22. ____
23. ____	20. ____	23. ____
24. ____	21. ____	24. ____
25. ____		25. ____
26. ____	22. ____	26. ____
27. ____		27. ____
28. ____		28. ____
29. ____		29. ____
30. ____		30. ____

In your view, with what success is this goal being achieved by our youth ministry?

AVERAGE OF ADULT WORKSHEET	AVERAGE OF YOUTH WORKSHEET	COMBINED AVERAGE
1. ____	1. ____	1. ____
2. ____	2. ____	2. ____
3. ____	3. ____	3. ____
4. ____	5. ____	4. ____
5. ____	4. ____	5. ____
6. ____		6. ____
7. ____		7. ____
8. ____	6. ____	8. ____
9. ____	7. ____	9. ____
10. ____	8. ____	10. ____
11. ____	9. ____	11. ____
12. ____	10. ____	12. ____
13. ____	12. ____	13. ____
14. ____	13. ____	14. ____
15. ____	11. ____	15. ____
16. ____	14. ____	16. ____
17. ____	15. ____	17. ____
18. ____	16. ____	18. ____
19. ____	17. ____	19. ____
20. ____		20. ____
21. ____	18. ____	21. ____
22. ____	19. ____	22. ____
23. ____	20. ____	23. ____
24. ____	21. ____	24. ____
25. ____		25. ____
26. ____	22. ____	26. ____
27. ____		27. ____
28. ____		28. ____
29. ____		29. ____
30. ____		30. ____

WORKSHEET 3: Parent Survey

Dear Parent,

Greetings! Your parish is very interested in learning more about its teenage members. A Youth Ministry Planning Team has been formed to develop a strong program for all high school students of the parish.

We need your help. Would you take a few minutes to answer the questions below? Your ideas are very important to our planning process. You do not have to sign your name.

Thank you.

1. If you have teenage children, what are their ages?

2. How do your teenagers spend their time?

3. What are some of the needs you think teenagers have?

4. How can the parish help?

5. Do you have particular suggestions for a youth ministry program?

6. General comments:

WORKSHEET 4: Youth Ministry Interview

NAME_____ INTERVIEWED BY_____

1. In your opinion, what are the particular needs of the youth in this community?

2. How could these needs be fulfilled?

3. What do you think a social group or church group could do to help fulfill their needs?

4. What are the positive characteristics of youth?

5. How could these characteristics be expanded, reinforced, supported?

6. Do you have any ideas for projects for youth?

7. Do you know of any youth group programs that have worked in the past in this parish or in other places?

8. General comments:

WORKSHEET 5: Planning Activity Form

OBJECTIVE:

ACTIVITY:

DATE: TIME:

LEADERS NEEDED: PLACE:

HELPERS NEEDED: RESOURCES, MATERIALS NEEDED:

IMPLEMENTATION STEPS:

METHOD OF EVALUATION:

WORSHEET 6: Program Planning Evaluation Worksheet

PART ONE: Checklist of Key Growth Points

I. Vision of Youth Ministry

_____ is understood in terms of its components and their interrelationships.

_____ is understood by all those presently involved in leading youth ministry in my parish or school, both youth and adults.

_____ is understood by those who must support the youth ministry effort (pastor, principal, parents, committee members, faculty).

_____ is understood by the youth involved in all dimensions of our youth ministry programs.

II. Administration and Organization for Youth Ministry

_____ is systematically undertaken in my parish or school with consideration for all aspects of youth ministry.

_____ is done cooperatively by a representative group.

_____ includes teens in the planning process.

III. Planning Steps for Youth Ministry

A. Needs

_____ What is already offered in the community has been analyzed.

_____ Needs, as youth see them, have been analyzed using several data-gathering methods.

_____ Needs, as adults see them, have been analyzed.

B. Data Analysis

_____ The information gathered about youth needs has been analyzed and conclusions drawn.

C. Goals

_____ An overall goal for our youth ministry efforts has been formulated . . .

_____ by a representative group . . .

_____ and has been presented to appropriate authorities (pastor, principal, parish council, faculty).

D. Plan

_____ A written plan including all dimensions of youth ministry has been put together to meet our goals.

E. **Procedures**

_____ Leadership has been recruited.

_____ Leadership has been trained.

_____ Programs have been publicized.

_____ Recruitment of youth has been planned.

_____ Space is available and planned for.

_____ Equipment and resources are available and planned for.

F. **Evaluation**

_____ Ongoing evaluation is formally conducted.

_____ Ongoing evaluation is informally conducted.

_____ Evaluation is used in planning the next stage of our work.

IV. **Community-Fellowship Setting for Youth Ministry**

_____ Our total plan provides for building community in all aspects of our ministry.

_____ Our total plan provides for specific settings for developing community (i.e., teen club, social events, etc.)

V. **Message/Study Settings for Youth Ministry**

_____ Our total plan provides opportunities for *evangelization,* including radical outreach and consideration of basic faith questions.

_____ Our total plan provides opportunities for *catechesis,* including occasional programs to reach those not ready for a week-by-week commitment.

_____ Our total plan provides in-depth development experiences for those who are ready (for example, study of prayer).

VI. **Service Settings for Youth Ministry**

_____ Our total plan provides ongoing opportunities for service, including needed training for youth.

_____ Our total plan provides short-term opportunities for service.

VII. **Worship Settings for Youth Ministry**

_____ Our total plan provides ongoing opportunities for youth liturgies.

_____ Our total plan provides ongoing opportunities for youth penance services.

_____ Our total plan provides ongoing opportunities for youth retreats.

_____ Our total plan provides ongoing opportunities for prayer and para-liturgical services.

_____ Our total plan provides ongoing opportunities for training youth in planning for and leading worship.

VIII. Special Interest Settings for Youth Ministry

_____ Our total plan provides for programs geared to the special interests and needs of teens, according to the needs analysis of our youth.

IX. Enablement

_____ Our total plan provides for leadership training for youth.

_____ Our total plan provides for needed training for adult leadership, according to role (catechists, counselors, coaches . . .).

_____ Our total plan provides for my own ongoing education and development in youth ministry.

X. Advocacy

_____ A youth committee (or subcommittee) exists, to represent youth concerns to the parish community.

_____ Staff members belong to and have contact with appropriate community groups, to represent youth needs.

_____ Staff members and youth workers listen to youth, and represent their needs and concerns to the parish and neighborhood community.

PART TWO: Resources to Help Our Youth Ministry Grow

A. Of the ten growth areas above, which two need most attention in our home setting now?

1.

2.

B. Of the ten, which two do you feel most able to facilitate?

1.

2.

C. Which two do you need most help with?

1.

2.

PART THREE: Action Steps to Help Our Youth Ministry Grow

A. What two action steps will you take to help our youth ministry grow?

1.

2.

B. What question do you have regarding these steps?

9
The Youth Minister As Enabler

The Importance of Volunteer Leaders

One of the essential responsibilities of the coordinator of youth ministry and the youth ministry team is to serve as a catalyst for the development of leaders (adult and youth) who share responsibility for the youth ministry. This is the work of enablement, a function which is crucial to the ongoing growth and development of youth ministry. The three stories which follow illustrate the ways in which a parish might encounter the need for a leadership system.

Scene 1: It had been a year since Karen had begun work at the parish as the full-time, professional youth minister. She had worked very hard to build up a youth program. It had been several years since the parish had had an organized youth program. Father Jim ran the program, but after he was transferred the program died. Initially Karen tried to get adult leaders involved in youth ministry, but nobody seemed to have the time. What she did find was a number of young people who wanted to see the church do something for them. Over the past year, Karen had developed a very sound youth ministry with increasing numbers of young people participating. She sponsored the Sunday evening youth gatherings, weekend retreats, short-term minicourses, seasonal worship experiences, and small-group bible study and prayer groups. She had developed such a good rapport with her youth that she was sought out by them for counseling and guidance. When she was not planning programs she was conducting them, or she was in her office counseling youth. She was beginning to feel that her ministry was a trap. She was entering a crisis in her ministry brought on by her effectiveness. She was coming to the realization that she could not maintain all the programs she had begun. She also realized that the youth ministry could not grow unless she got some help. Fast!

Scene 2: The youth ministry team had worked long and hard to plan and implement a youth ministry in the parish. The team was organized by several concerned parishioners with the blessings of the pastor. They had talked to resource people and visited other parishes to determine the best way to start a youth ministry. They then set out to work through the steps of the program planning: assessing needs, prioritizing needs, writing objectives based on the needs, developing programs based on the objectives. Now they had come to their final meeting; tonight all their hard work would bear fruit. As each committee reported on the programs that they had developed for the coming year it became more and more obvious that the resources of the youth ministry team would be hard pressed to implement and staff all of these programs. Adults and youth on the team began to wonder if months of planning would end in frustrated dreams because of a lack of leaders.

Scene 3: Bill had just been hired by the parish to serve as the full-time professional youth minister. Last year Father Steve and a handful of adults had organized the youth ministry in cooperation with the youth group. Father Steve was too busy this year to be involved, so the parish decided to hire a youth minister. Father Steve, the adult leaders, and the young people are hoping that Bill will continue the good work that has already begun. Upon close examination of the youth ministry, Bill discovered how unorganized the youth program really was. In his discussions with the adult leaders he recognized signs of frustration and tiredness—there were too few adults involved and they were running "dry." In his discussion with the parish staff and the adult leaders, Bill got the distinct impression that he was hired to take the "burden" of the youth program off the shoulders of staff and adult leaders. Yet to maintain existing programs and develop new directions for youth ministry, Bill needed to involve new adult leaders. He also needed to involve young people in the active planning for youth ministry. Bill was caught in a tension between the need to broaden the youth ministry and its leadership base, while meeting the expectations of the staff, youth, and adult leaders. Could he find a way to develop new leaders and new styles of planning, while retaining his veteran leaders and meeting the expectations of those who hired him?

Each of these stories, though different, points to a similar crisis—a crisis of growth and leadership. Because of her effectiveness Karen needs to broaden the leadership base of her ministry by involving new leaders. Because of their diligence in planning, the youth ministry team has developed a comprehensive ministry that requires a cadre of leaders which goes beyond their team. Because of poor planning and too few leaders, Bill must organize the youth ministry and add new leaders, while retaining the support of his veteran leaders and parish staff. Each is facing a crisis that can be solved. By developing an enabling style of leadership and creating a leader development system, all three parishes can deal with this crisis and grow. All too often it is at this point that youth ministers give up, overwhelmed by the prospect of finding leaders.

This chapter and the next one introduce a philosophy and a series of procedures for sustaining volunteers in youth ministry.

Understanding Enablement

Enablement may be a crucial aspect of ministry; however, it is also—despite all best intentions—quite difficult to practice.

James Fenhagen, in his book *Mutual Ministry,* writes:

The concept of "ministry of enablement" is firmly rooted in the New Testament understanding of the Church's mission. The way in which Jesus empowered his disciples for their ministry had the effect of enabling them to exercise ministries that built on the unique gifts which each possessed. . . .

It is in the Epistle to the Ephesians, however, that our charge is more clearly stated. "And these were his gifts," states the writer, "some to be apostles, some prophets, some evangelists, some pastors and teachers, to equip God's people for work in his service, to the building up of the body of Christ" (Ephesians 4:11–14). The task of the Church's ministry is to equip one another so that all might live as Christ's servants in the world. The key is "equip" which in its root form refers to the "building up" of the body, the community of faith, and the "spiritual strengthening" necessary for the "service of Christ" in the world. The word "enablement" has a similar meaning, although coming from a different root. Enablement refers to the process by which we make it possible for others to find both the strength and authority to fulfill the purposes of their lives. As the *laos* — the People of God, ordained and not ordained — we have been sent into the world to exercise ministry according to the gifts given us by the Spirit. . . . Every member of the body possesses the gift necessary for ministry. The task of the congregation, therefore, is to enable these gifts to be put to use.[1]

This understanding of the Church and the universal call to exercise one's gifts by virtue of one's baptism is well grounded in Vatican II and post–Vatican II theology. Yet this work of enablement is often rare in practice. Many parishes still labor under the concept of the minister (be it the pastor, DRE, or youth minister) as one who is hired primarily to "do ministry" on behalf of others (children, youth, adults, or the entire community). This minister is expected to be all things to all people all the time. It is often a traumatic transition for community and minister to develop a style of leadership which is primarily enabling.

Fenhagen continues:

Enablement has to do with the genuine sharing of gifts. It involves mutual support and accountability as everyone seeks to exercise his or her particular function of ministry. For a pastor (or youth minister) to help bring this about (and it won't happen unless he or she is committed to at least giving it a try) there must be not only a high degree of security, but genuine skill and the ability to see things through.[2]

Fenhagen identifies four major attitudinal and value changes that need to occur if there is to be a genuine ministry of enablement:

1) It is more important for the ministers [i.e., leaders] in a congregation to enable others to identify and carry out their ministries than to do it themselves.

    The best use of the skills of the "professional" is to extend the ministry through others. This is not only theologically sound but a very practical and efficient use of the resources that are available to us.

2) Recruiting persons for ministry is only half the task. Without consistent and ongoing support — the hard follow-through — enablement will not take place.

3) Interdependence is preferable to dependence. The task of [the leader] is to enable persons to move from dependence on them and what they symbolize to genuine interdependent behavior both in church and outside. This involves not only giving help to others but being able to ask help for ourselves.

4) The greatest gift a [minister] has to give another is not the right answer but the authenticity of his or her own search. This is enabling. As Henri Nouwen has written, "When the imitation of Christ does not mean to live a life like Christ, but to live our life as authentically as Christ lived his, then there are many ways and forms in which a [person] can be a Christian. The minister is the one who can make this search for authenticity possible, not by standing on the side as a neutral screen or an impartial observer, but as an articulate witness of Christ, who puts his or her own search at the disposal of others."[3]

The ministry of enablement is not a program but a process. It means calling forth the faith and giftedness of the community and placing those gifts in service to the community and world. This means placing high priority on the development and support of the total ministry of the faith community. It also means developing an organizational model of youth ministry which is enabling — thus the need for a leader development system.

What Is a Leader Development System?

A *leader development system*[4] is the youth ministry's comprehensive plan for enlisting, training, and supporting all its designated leaders, a system in which all the functions and tasks are clearly defined, delegated, and related to one another. A system is the whole design or strategy for getting things done. All the parts in it are clearly related to the other parts. This concept of a "system" for leader development is often foreign to those in youth ministry. They may have been accustomed to a rather unplanned way of "recruiting" leaders. In many youth ministries, people work at one or another aspect of leader development without reference to an overall plan. By contrast, the leader development system provides a disciplined approach to the three major components of developing leaders: enlisting them, training them, and providing them with supervision and support.

The process of *enlisting* leaders involves deciding just which leaders will be needed for the youth ministry programs and identifying the people who might serve in those areas. Then these persons are invited to serve, and an agreement is worked out with them about the terms of their leadership.

The *training* component provides newly enlisted leaders with pre-service training experiences, helping them to gain the skills and understanding they need in order to serve effectively. Once they are on the job, training continues by helping them to discover those areas where they need still further growth, and then arranging for appropriate in-service training.

The third part of the system is *supervising* and *supporting* leaders. While they are on the job, support and counsel helps leaders to improve their performance. "Supervision" is not used here in the sense of administering a program or directing the work of subordinates; rather, it is an educational function in which one person helps another to discover how he or she can take steps to grow in particular areas of leadership.

In a system all the parts are related to one another. Nothing is "left over." Nothing operates "by itself." In this book the system of leader development has been organized into five closely related steps. They are presented in detail in chapter 10, but their basic interrelationships are described below.

STEP 1: *Describing needed leadership positions* is the first of three steps pertaining to enlisting leaders. At this point the task is to analyze planned activities to determine how many leaders will be needed, with what kinds of skills and talents. The programs determine the leadership needs. This analysis lends to the writing of simple but complete "job descriptions" that will provide a basis for recruiting leaders, training them, and supervising them.

STEP 2: *Identifying potential leaders* is the community-wide search for individuals with the time, ability, and willingness to fill the leadership roles that were named in Step 1. This is an information-gathering phase.

STEP 3: *Securing needed leaders* is the stage at which actual personal recruitment is conducted. Using the job description as the basis for discussion, the volunteers and recruiters can agree on the specifics of an assignment.

STEP 4: *Training of leaders* can be planned as soon as the enlistment phase is complete. Training is called for when there is a gap between the qualifications of the volunteer and the specific demands of the leadership role he or she will be assuming. The training can be minimal or in-depth, pre-service or at occasional intervals throughout service.

STEP 5: *Supporting leaders* involves the ongoing contact that keeps the coordinator or team in touch with the volunteers. Someone is designated to help each volunteer solve problems and grow in leadership. Support also means affirming and celebrating the contributions of volunteer leaders to the church's youth ministry.

Designing and Managing the System

Although the steps involved in leadership development are clear, there is a lot of leeway available for actual implementation. Different options are included in the process, with the assumption that the youth ministry coordinator or team will set up a system that is best suited to their particular circumstances. After the design is set up, the system will have to be managed by the coordinator and/or the team. (A goal to strive for is the active involvement of the youth ministry team in carrying out leader development tasks.)

In managing the system the coordinator and the team may do more planning, set up specific targets and goals, enlist persons and groups to implement certain aspects of the system (e.g., a recruitment task force), see that these people have the training and resources they need and, in general, make sure that all parts of the system are carried out, evaluated, and improved as needed.

Two preliminary projects are recommended before designing a parish leadership development plan: one is assessing the current state of leadership in the youth ministry program; the other is examining some other resources for information on leadership development.

Assessing Current Leader Development

There are two different procedures found at the end of this chapter to help a youth ministry team assess its current leader development situation. "Leader Development in Youth Ministry" is an assessment instrument that can provide a measure of the parish's performance in thirty-five areas of leader development. The questionnaire is particularly useful because it can also be used as a final evaluation instrument when the system has been completed and is in operation. The "Present Leadership Analysis" is the second procedure for reviewing the status of youth ministry leadership. Both parts of this assessment have an accompanying worksheet created to answer questions such as: "What leadership jobs are currently held by volunteers? What are the functions involved in these roles? What abilities and skills are needed to do them? Who are the leaders? What do they do? What do they know? What skills do they have? How well are they doing? How do they feel about their work? What is the response from the youth?" (This second procedure is especially helpful for coordinators who find themselves in an established youth ministry which needs organization and leader development.)

Further Resources

The list below contains nine recommended resources that can be consulted for further information on volunteer development.

Johnson, Douglas. *The Care and Feeding of Volunteers.* Nashville: Abingdon Press, 1978. $4.95.

Lindgren, Alvin J., and Norman Shawchuck. *Let My People Go: Empowering Laity for Ministry.* Nashville: Abingdon Press, 1980. $5.95.

Rauner, Judy. *Helping People Volunteer.* San Diego: Marlborough Publications, 1980. Write to: Marlborough Publications, P.O. Box 16406, San Diego, CA. Highly recommended. $10.00.

Schaller, Lyle E. "Who Nurtures the Volunteers in Your Parish?" *PACE* 13 (1982–1983): Community–E. $2.00.

Scheitlin, George, and Eleanore Gillstrom. *Recruiting and Developing Volunteer Leaders.* Philadelphia: Parish Life Press, 1979. $4.00.

Schindler-Rainman, Eva, and Ronald Lippit. *The Volunteer Community.* La Jolla, CA: University Associates, 1977. $9.50.

Stenzel, Anne K., and Helen M. Feeney. *Volunteer Training and Development: A Manual.* Rev. ed. New York: Seabury Press, 1976. $12.95.

United Church of Christ, Office of Church Life and Leadership. *The Ministry of Volunteers: A Guidebook for Churches.* Seven vols. in ring binder. St. Louis: United Church of Christ, 1979. $25.00.

Wilson, Marlene. *The Effective Management of Volunteer Programs.* Boulder, CO: Volunteer Management Associates, 1976. Write to: Volunteer Management Associates, 279 South Cedarbrook Road, Boulder, CO 80302. Also available through University Associates, La Jolla, CA. $9.50.

WORKSHEET 7: Leader Development in Youth Ministry

This assessment instrument is designed to: (a) involve people in an evaluation process, (b) give credit for what is already working well, and (c) help determine what is needed to improve effectiveness. You may identify a need that is not covered in this survey. Add your own, please.

It may be difficult to decide which column applies to your situation. The responses are value judgments. The process of sharing opinions increases validity of the assessment results.

Here are suggested guidelines for the response options:

YES: We do this: our success could range from "outstanding" to "fair."
PLANNED: We plan to do this: concrete plans exist to implement this in the near future.
NEEDED: We need to work on this: we are aware of the need, but have no current plan to implement it.
NOT NEEDED: We do not need this: at this time we could function well without it.

Check the column that reflects your current evaluation of your leader development system.

Enlisting leaders	FAIR			OUTSTANDING	PLANNED	NEEDED	NOT NEEDED
1. We list all the settings for our congregation's ministry where leaders will be needed.	1	2	3	4	5	___	___	___
2. We describe each of these settings in writing.	1	2	3	4	5	___	___	___
3. We list the tasks which all the needed leaders of these settings will perform.	1	2	3	4	5	___	___	___
4. We list all the positions for which leaders will be needed.	1	2	3	4	5	___	___	___

Enlisting leaders

	FAIR				OUTSTANDING			
	1	2	3	4	5	PLANNED	NEEDED	NOT NEEDED
5. We write a job description for each leadership position.	1	2	3	4	5	—	—	—
6. We frequently interpret to the congregation the meaning and opportunity of Christian leadership in youth ministry.	1	2	3	4	5	—	—	—
7. We search continually for persons with leadership potential. There is an ongoing process of recruitment.	1	2	3	4	5	—	—	—
8. Periodically we survey the congregation to discover leadership abilities and interests.	1	2	3	4	5	—	—	—
9. We maintain an up-to-date file with information about potential leaders.	1	2	3	4	5	—	—	—
10. We select each prospective leader based on thorough knowledge of both the job and the prospect.	1	2	3	4	5	—	—	—
11. We invite each prospect through personal contact and thoroughly explain the responsibility involved.	1	2	3	4	5	—	—	—

12. With each enlisted leader, we establish a clear agreement regarding the responsibilities and terms of his or her service.

    1   2   3   4   5

13. We enlist 100 percent of the leaders needed to carry out the planned ministries of our congregation.

    1   2   3   4   5

Training leaders

14. We provide new leaders with sufficient orientation to their work.

    1   2   3   4   5

15. We help all leaders—new or already serving—to diagnose their needs for training and growth.

    1   2   3   4   5

16. We help each leader set specific goals for his or her own training and growth.

    1   2   3   4   5

17. We help leaders locate the training they need to reach their goals, or we provide this training for them.

    1   2   3   4   5

18. All leaders participate in the training opportunities they need.

    1   2   3   4   5

19. Every training event in which leaders engage is 100 percent effective in helping them reach their goals.

    1   2   3   4   5

Supervising leaders

	FAIR				OUTSTANDING	PLANNED	NEEDED	NOT NEEDED
20. Each new leader is authorized to begin service by an official leader of the community.	1	2	3	4	5	—	—	—
21. For each leader there is a designated supervisor who will provide support and guidance.	1	2	3	4	5	—	—	—
22. Each leader and supervisor communicates regularly and openly.	1	2	3	4	5	—	—	—
23. Each leader participates regularly in a face-to-face group which supports and guides him or her.	1	2	3	4	5	—	—	—
24. Each leader participates fully in the life of the faith community.	1	2	3	4	5	—	—	—
25. Each leader participates responsibly in the life of the community and the wider world.	1	2	3	4	5	—	—	—
26. We provide all leaders with the resources and information they need for their work.	1	2	3	4	5	—	—	—
27. Each leader and supervisor gathers information about the leader's work and evaluates his or her leadership.	1	2	3	4	5	—	—	—

	1	2	3	4	5			
28. With the supervisor's help, each leader is continually growing and improving in leadership.	1	2	3	4	5			
29. We express to each leader the congregation's appreciation and support, and occasionally celebrate this in worship.	1	2	3	4	5			
30. Each leader is recognized and thanked at the conclusion of service.	1	2	3	4	5			

Design and management

	1	2	3	4	5			
31. Those in our youth ministry responsible for leader development are clearly designated.	1	2	3	4	5			
32. These groups and persons are operating regularly and effectively.	1	2	3	4	5			
33. We have developed a comprehensive system or design for enlisting, training, and supervising our leaders.	1	2	3	4	5			
34. All aspects of this system are operating fully and effectively.	1	2	3	4	5			
35. We evaluate our work in leader development regularly and thoroughly.	1	2	3	4	5			

Present Leadership Analysis

PART I: Present Leadership Positions
(This is a sample. Blank worksheet on next page.)

Leadership jobs (list all)	Functions of each job	Abilities and special skills needed for each job	Special knowledge needed for each job
Catechist	1. Facilitator of learning 2. Guide and counselor 3. Mediator and interpreter of Christian faith 4. Link with community	1. Plan and conduct learning experiences 2. Demonstrate loving concern for youth 3. Teach in accordance with educational goals of total Church	1. Basic understanding of age group being taught 2. Acquaintance with historical and current theology 3. Awareness of educational goals of the congregation 4. Understanding of learning theory
Youth group advisor	1. Friend and guide of youth 2. Chaperone 3. Leader of youth activities	1. Love for youth 2. Personal maturity 3. Initiative and self-direction 4. Willingness and skill to be in relationship with youth	1. Basic understanding of age group 2. Communication skills 3. Knowledge of youth culture

WORKSHEET 8: Present Leadership Analysis

PART I: Present Leadership Positions

Leadership jobs (list all)	Functions of each job	Abilities and special skills needed for each job	Special knowledge needed for each job

Present Leadership Analysis

PART II: Present Leaders

Present leaders	Jobs held by each leader	Kinds of knowledge each has	Kinds of skills each has	Degree of competence in each skill	Youth's response to each other	Attitude of leader toward present role

Notes

1. James Fenhagen, *Mutual Ministry* (New York: Seabury Press, 1977), pp. 99–100.

2. Ibid., p. 104.

3. Ibid., pp. 105–106.

4. This definition and discussion of "leadership development system" has been adapted from *Leader Development Resource System,* a series of pamphlets published by the Board of Discipleship, United Methodist Church, 1972.

10
Five Steps to Developing Volunteer Leaders

Welcome to a "workshop" chapter on the nuts-and-bolts of managing a leadership development system. Each step of the process is explained in detail in this chapter, providing the practical "how-to's" of each task along with helpful worksheets. The style is direct and informal; it is addressed to you, the reader, so that you can work along with the material as you design your own leadership system.

STEP 1: Describing Needed Leadership Positions

Describing programs for which leaders will be needed

Based on the programs you have projected for the coming year and those you already have in existence, list all the programs for which leaders will be needed. Also include leadership needs in the area of administration. If you have used the "Planning Activity Form" from chapter 8, you will already have all the pertinent information needed: objective, nature of the program, nature and number of participants, times of meeting and duration, implementation steps, place, possible resources, and so on. Obtaining this information is essential if you are to define the tasks of leadership and the number of leadership positions you need for each program.

Listing tasks which needed leaders will perform

Now identify the leadership tasks which must be performed for each program that will need leaders. Listing the different *tasks* associated with the program comes prior to listing *positions*. Often we list positions first only to find that the number of leadership tasks far outnumbers the positions we have created. This problem leads to frustration and burnout in the leaders we have recruited and placed in service to youth. By starting with the leadership tasks we can define more precisely the number of leadership positions needed and what each position demands.

Listing positions for which leaders will be needed

Using the program descriptions and the list of leader tasks, it is now possible to decide what leadership positions are needed for each program. Worksheets

9 and 10 combine the work of these three tasks and help to prepare for the writing of job descriptions.

Writing job descriptions

For each needed leadership position that was outlined, a description of the job needs to be developed, including the following information: tasks to be performed, skills and abilities needed, schedule and length of service, arrangements for supervision and training. These job descriptions will be the guide for all other areas of leader development: securing leaders, supervising and supporting leaders, training leaders, and evaluating leaders' work. The job descriptions serve as the basis of agreement between you and your leaders. Job descriptions should be organized into a permanent file with the corresponding "Planning Activity Form" (see chapter 8, Worksheet 5). In this way the hard work you have completed can be used for years to come.

Worksheet 11 provides you with a way to develop a job description for each leadership position. Here are several guidelines to follow in developing the job description. They correspond to the categories of the worksheet.

1) Identify the program the leader will be involved in. If the job has a title, state it.
2) List the leader tasks to be performed. Use open-ended and creative sentences rather than binding statements. Describe what you hope will be accomplished. Use clear, simple language.
3) Identify the abilities needed by the person who will be doing the job. If you are not entirely sure what skills and knowledge are needed, consult other leaders in youth ministry or in your particular area of concern. (For example, if you are not sure what abilities are needed for leading a retreat, consult with experienced retreat leaders. If you are not sure what is involved in teaching, consult a professional religious educator. This would also hold true if you were not sure about the tasks to be performed. Consult with resource people.) Simple, direct, minimum abilities should be identified. Try not to overwhelm people, yet be honest about the abilities that are needed. Remember, your training program can help a person with good potential to develop the needed abilities.
4) Clearly state the total involvement that goes with the job, e.g., a retreat coordinator may also be expected to be a member of the youth ministry team.
5) Identify the length of commitment. Be specific. In determining the length of commitment, compute the hours of direct service to youth plus time for planning meetings, training sessions, support-guidance groups, and other peripheral activities. A teacher who is willing to teach a six-week minicourse needs to know that he or she is expected to participate in two teacher meetings and two training sessions. A job

description should include the total commitment. Many leaders become angry and frustrated when they realize a six-week commitment really means a twelve-week involvement.

6) Identify the supervision and support which will be provided for the leader.

7) If specific training is required for the position, list the training requirements. Identify when and how the training may be secured.

8) Identify what the leader will gain from this position. What are the benefits of this position?

9) Clearly identify to whom the leader is responsible.

WORKSHEET 9: Describing Needed Leadership Positions

Program	Leadership Tasks	Needed Leadership Position
A. _____	1. _____	Position: _____
	2. _____	(Task #'s _____)
	3. _____	Position: _____
	4. _____	(Task #'s _____)
	5. _____	Position: _____
	6. _____	(Task #'s _____)
	7. _____	
B. _____	1. _____	Position: _____
	2. _____	(Task #'s _____)
	3. _____	Position: _____
	4. _____	(Task #'s _____)
	5. _____	
	6. _____	

(Make additional sheets as needed)

WORKSHEET 10: Summary of Leadership Needs

Fill in this sheet with the leadership positions identified with the aid of the preceding worksheet. This summary provides an overview of recruitment needs.

Leadership positions	Program	Leaders okay "as is"	Leaders need training	New leaders needed

WORKSHEET 11: Leader's Job Description

1. Component of Youth Ministry:

   _____

   Program: _____

   Job title: _____

2. Leader Tasks to Be Performed:

   1.
   2.
   3.
   4.
   5.
   6.
   7.
   8.
   9.
   10.

3. Abilities Needed:
   (skills, attitudes, understanding)

   1.
   2.
   3.
   4.
   5.
   6.
   7.
   8.
   9.
   10.

4. Involvement:

   Other commitments:

   Additional responsibilities:

   Additional meetings:

5. Length of Commitment:

   Service: from _____ to _____

   Meetings:

   Training:

6. Supervision:

   Who provides: _____

   When: _____

   Support:

   Who provides: _____

   When/meetings: _____

7. Training Required:

   When and how training can be secured:

8. Benefits of the Position
   to the Leader:

9. Responsible to: _____

Completed by _____

Date _____

STEP 2: Identifying Potential Leaders

This function of the leader development system is commonly referred to as "recruitment." Recruitment is far more than simply finding the right person for a job. It involves educating the parish community to youth ministry and the opportunities for service in youth ministry, as well as gathering the essential information for securing leaders. It is a year-round task.

Interpreting Christian leadership as an opportunity

Share with all members of the parish community the meaning of service as a Christian leader — its motivation, responsibility, and rewards. "Spread the Good Word" through personal conversation; through presentations to groups; from the pulpit; in written form through brochures, newsletters, and bulletin announcements; and by displays and posters. Interpreting youth ministry as an opportunity for Christian service is a year-round task. It involves continually educating the parish community.

Some of the specific ways in which youth ministers have promoted opportunities for service in youth ministry are as follows:

Parish newsletter and/or bulletin: Many youth ministers have developed monthly youth ministry newsletters to communicate to the youth and adult community what is happening in youth ministry. This offers a vehicle to interpret leadership needs to potential adult leaders. Many parishes have a parishwide monthly or quarterly newsletter. This offers the youth minister an opportunity to promote youth ministry and to describe the opportunities for service in youth ministry. The bulletin is another vehicle of communication, if used correctly.

The one thing you *do not* want to do is place one of those "pleading" announcements, begging the adult community to get involved in youth ministry. These announcements let the adults know that if they do not get involved there will be no youth program for their youth. Usually what these announcements produce is exactly the opposite of their intention. Adults who are not qualified or who feel "guilty" are attracted to the youth ministry. You do not need this type of leader. Furthermore, this type of bulletin announcement is an insult to your hard-working dedicated adults who consider youth ministry a calling. Instead, use the bulletin to educate about youth ministry. Try to get a regular column in the bulletin. When you are looking for new leaders, write a "want ad," giving plenty of information and telling the prospective leader whom to contact for further details. You might run a "want ad" weekly, based on needed leadership positions.

Brochures: An attractive and very professional way of communicating youth ministry and the opportunities for leadership is through a brochure. The brochure describes needed leadership positions and the responsibilities of each position. You might list each leadership position in a paragraph, describing the required tasks, needed abilities, and time commitment. Be sure to include an application in the brochure asking the prospects to list their abilities, background information, what positions they would be interested in, and so on.

You can distribute these brochures at all the Sunday Masses and request that those who are interested in serving or who desire more information drop the application form in a special box as they leave Mass. You can then follow up each application with a phone call and a personal visit. The brochure can also be used by the recruiter or recruiting team when it contacts prospective leaders. The brochure can be given to the prospect and used to match the individual's gifts with a leadership position. The brochure communicates the value you place on leaders and also provides the recruiter with a concrete visual to augment his or her presentation.

Displays and posters: You can utilize an attractive poster to announce leadership opportunities. The poster can be part of a youth ministry display which communicates what is happening in the youth ministry, as well as what leadership opportunities presently exist. This display can be set up permanently (in a particular place in the church) or assembled weekly. In addition to the poster and/or display, you and your team might want to develop a multimedia presentation with slides, music, conversation, interviews, commentary, and photos on youth ministry and the parish programs for youth. Include in this presentation information on leadership opportunities. You can take this presentation to parish organizations and small group meetings. It can also serve as an excellent orientation for new young people and new, or prospective, leaders.

Presentations: You and your team might want to schedule presentations at parish meetings to discuss youth ministry and the opportunities for service. You might also want to organize small group meetings for prospective leaders convened by your key adult leaders at their homes. Also, you can convene a parishwide meeting to present the direction of youth ministry and the opportunities for service. This last option is the most difficult to organize effectively. With good promotion it can work very well. It might be best scheduled after you have distributed your brochures and invited adults to attend the meeting to explore further opportunities for service.

In each of these options you can use your display, posters, and/or multimedia presentation to effectively communicate youth ministry. Be sure to have members of your team (especially the youth leaders) discuss youth ministry at these meetings. It is an effective sign to prospective leaders when they see adults and youth excited about youth ministry.

Searching for persons with leadership potential

Look and listen twelve months a year for persons who should be considered for leadership positions. True, you have immediate need for leaders so that new programs can be implemented. However, many programs do not begin at the same time—they are initiated at various times throughout the year. Thus there is a need for leaders throughout the year. Because most parishes have both immediate and long-range needs for leaders, it is important to see the recruitment effort as a continuing process. Also, since potential leaders are always surfacing, you should be continually searching out and developing a list of potential leaders.

Marlene Wilson, in *The Effective Management of Volunteer Programs,* lists several specific suggestions for searching out potential leaders:

1) Do specific rather than general recruiting, whenever possible. [Job descriptions will aid you in this task, as will a brochure.]

2) Choose appropriate audiences whose interests and priorities match your needs. [Look to renewal programs, adult education programs, and professional youth workers for potential leaders.]

3) Determine where the skills are that you need and actively seek them out. If you wait for volunteers to find out instead of actively seeking them out, the results will usually be disappointing.

4) Be as specific and honest in your appeal as possible. [Your job descriptions should help you to do this. Clearly state what the job involves and how much time it requires. In many ways you are "selling" the position. You are trying to link the person's interests, gifts, and skills to the positions for which you need leaders.]

5) Be sure to utilize existing information. [Check out the parish census, time and talent survey, prospective leaders recommended by the parish staff, current adult leaders, youth, and names of prospects from leaders in other parish ministries and organizations.]

6) Recruit by inviting people to respond to the opportunity to be of service, not by telling them they ought to be concerned and involved. [If the jobs that have been designed are meaningful, you should be able to enthusiastically approach your parish community with a real offer to serve, to grow, and to make a difference in the lives of young people.]

7) Be enthusiastic! [If you and your team are not committed to or excited about the youth ministry, no one else will be either. And most certainly, lack of enthusiam will not attract or inspire leaders to want to serve.][1]

Surveying for leadership abilities and interests

In addition to the more focused approach to recruitment you may also want to plan a general survey of all the members of the parish community in order to discover other potential leaders. This project is best conducted as a joint venture of the entire parish staff, or at least as a cooperative project between the youth minister and DRE. Surveying leadership abilities and interests may involve finding or developing questionnaires, conducting a survey, recording the information received, and thanking all who respond. The amount of experience, gifts, talents, skills, and understanding should also be registered, along with the expression of interest.

The following are some suggestions to guide the persons responsible for surveying the talents, interests, and experiences of the members of the parish.

1) None of the information gathered should be confidential; all workers in the church should have access to the records.

2) Sometimes confidential information is needed to supplement the information on file; therefore, the records should contain references, the names of persons with whom each individual has worked (professional and volunteer workers in the local church, community workers, et al.).

3) Avoid requests for information that are too intricate; include only what is essential.

4) More than the "run-of-the-mill" information should be included; the creativity of an increasing number of persons is ready for release.

5) Provide an opportunity to indicate interest in more than the usual jobs; include provisions for checking interest in initiating new forms of education, serving as a member of planning and evaluation teams, working with others to initiate new forms of justice ministry, and other activities.

6) Many persons will serve if given an opportunity for training. A place for stating the desire for training should be provided.

7) Avoid making too much comparison between academic training and non-academic background. Make evident the importance of experience, self-study, personal and spiritual growth.

8) Provide an opportunity for registering attitudes and understanding: role of the leader, most effective teaching methods, most effective ways to communicate with youth.

9) Remember that an increasing variety of talents is being made available through the early retirement of persons in the Church and community.

Your survey can focus only on youth ministry or provide an even larger contribution to the parish by including all ministries. If you choose a broad-based survey, be sure to work with the parish staff members in its design and implementation.

Worksheet 12 is provided as an example which you can refer to as you create your own survey.

Developing a file of potential leaders

Organize the information from the searching and surveying in a permanent, up-to-date file of potential leaders. This involves designing a filing system, securing or developing forms on which to record the information, and keep-

ing all information current and useful for those who must select prospective leaders for particular positions.

There are several ways to store the information you receive; three of the simplest and least expensive ways are (1) loose-leaf notebook system, (2) card file system, and (3) summary assessment forms.

Loose-leaf notebook system: It is recommended that you develop three notebooks. One notebook should contain all the forms of those who returned the survey, listing interests, talents, experience, and training. A second notebook would list the leadership positions needed and the names of persons available for them. A third notebook would contain the youth ministry's statement of objectives and plans for the year; descriptions of the programs; the skills, attitudes, and understandings needed for each position; and a description of each job to be done (job descriptions). In short, the three notebooks allow you to organize all your work in leader development into a very easy-to-use system.

Card file system: Information is gathered on file cards and then sorted into two categories: (1) an alphabetical listing of those who returned the survey indicating their talents, interests, and services; and (2) a listing of the jobs that need doing, with the names of each member interested, experienced, and committed to doing them. A third category of information can also be stored recording the services and activities in which persons have participated. Under these services there should be a record of the date of participation in the service activity. A similar record should be made of the training received and references—names of persons with whom each individual has worked.

Summary assessment forms: Worksheet 13 provides a format for recording information about potential leaders.

WORKSHEET 12: Dedication of Time and Talents

Realizing that my time and talents must be made available if the Church is to responsibly fulfill its call to be engaged in continuing the mission and ministry of Jesus Christ, I hereby indicate my desire to dedicate a portion of my time and services to youth ministry in the area(s) checked in the following listings. I understand that assignment to any specific tasks will be made only after appropriate consultation and with prayerful deliberation.

(Please check ALL the areas you would be willing to serve in. You may indicate preferences by using numbers instead of just a check mark.)

Name _____ Phone _____

Address _____

Age: 20s _____ 30s _____ 40s _____ 50s _____ 60s _____ 70s _____

Occupation _____ Business address _____

Business phone _____

List special training _____

_____

Hobbies _____

Interests _____

Active in what church ministries _____

Active in what non-church organizations _____

Participating in what community activities _____

I would be glad to serve in youth ministry in the area(s) of:

_____ Teaching _____ Prayer leader _____ Retreat leader

_____ Adult advisor _____ Organization, planning _____ Service

_____ Justice and peace _____ Social activities _____ Athletic activities

Time you have available for youth ministry:

　　　Hours per week _____

　　　Regularly each week: _____ Yes _____ No

　　　Almost any time: _____ Yes _____ No

　　　Any preferred days or evenings _____

WORKSHEET 13: Assessment of Potential Leaders

Persons' names	Each person's skills, competencies, and qualities	Present leadership roles in the community	Possible motivations of each person	Possible positions in youth ministry

STEP 3: Securing Needed Leaders

The task of matching the needs of youth ministry leaders to the skills and
abilities of the potential leaders can begin when the tasks of *describing needed
leadership positions* and *identifying potential leaders* have been completed.
We have now compiled job descriptions for all the leadership positions in each
program. We have developed a list of potential leaders with their skills, abilities,
background, and experience. We have also developed a system to file this information for retrieval. We can now move on to the task of matching needs
and talents.

Selecting prospective volunteers

First examine the list of positions that need to be filled. Then study each person carefully, in light of his or her interests, abilities, limitations, and potential. Place the person's name opposite the need(s) he or she could be meeting
or the job(s) that could be filled. Some people will appear in several places.
Some will appear only once. Some will be placed opposite tasks which can
only be filled if he or she takes the necessary training.

It is now possible to balance all the leadership needs of youth ministry
with all the skills and abilities available within the parish. Each person can
now be located in a leadership role where his or her skills and interests enrich
and expand the youth ministry.

Choose one or more prospects for each position, ranking them if desired.
Lastly, decide whether each person will be invited to (a) explore the possibility of service as a leader, (b) engage in training for service, or (c) actually
begin service.

When both lists are finished and a serious attempt at matching has taken
place, there will probably be two pieces of the puzzle unsolved: (1) There
will be an "excess" of resources and skills not assigned to any job. (An excep-
tional and happy problem.) (2) There will also be "unfilled jobs." (Our usual
situation.)

It should not be a major problem to create new programs or to strengthen
your existing leadership teams now assigned to programs or to strengthen your
administrative team with the "excess" of resources and skills not assigned.

However, the task of finding people to fill unfilled jobs demands creativity and a renewed effort. You may need to retrace your steps, hoping to locate
potential leaders that you missed the first time. You may need to prioritize
your existing programs to make sure the most important programs are staffed.
But before you drop any important programs, remember there is an untapped
resource available to you—community leaders.

Most communities have persons and agencies with specific skills and
resources that could fill your leadership needs. For example, you may need
a leader to organize service projects for the coming year. Not finding anyone,
you might give up or take on the responsibility yourself. (Neither of these is

a desirable alternative.) Instead, research your community. Locate service placements for your youth (this can be done with young people assisting you) and develop a contact person in each placement. These professionals and paraprofessionals can serve as placement contacts, orient youth who are interested in serving in the organization, and provide the training needed to perform leadership tasks. The roles of the coordinator of youth ministry and the team would be to develop and maintain the relationships with these contact people and to place young people in a position of their choice. One parish which used this approach to leadership development found that many of these contact people were parishioners. They not only implemented an important program, but involved well over a dozen adults from the parish in the process.

Community agencies and professionals can also provide you with valuable counseling services. Also, many organizations provide lists of speakers who can be of help in setting up a program. By locating the right community resources you can fulfill many leadership responsibilities.

Lastly, many youths and young adults can capably serve as leaders if they are called forth and provided training. Do not overlook the potential of youth and young adults as you select prospects. Oftentimes the leaders you need are simply waiting to be called upon.

Gathering further information on prospects

In some cases you will need still more information about a prospective leader — about his or her background, experience, interests, abilities, attitudes, availability, and so on. If so, converse with the prospect, or perhaps interview the person in a more formal way. Worksheet 14 provides an exercise that a prospective leader can complete in order to focus on his or her specific gifts.

Inviting prospects to explore, train, or serve

The next step is to contact each prospect personally. This means using the job description that has been developed as a guide for explaining the details of the particular leadership position. It means inviting the prospect to explore such service, to train for service, or to actually begin service.

It is at this point that you must determine how to contact each prospect and what to say. The most effective vehicle for recruiting leaders is the "recruiting team." Too often the coordinator of youth ministry is left with the burden of having to contact potential leaders, meet with them one-on-one, and try to convince them to use their gifts and talents in youth ministry. Often the youth minister has no relationship with these prospects. Many prospects may feel that you are trying to recruit them to do a job which belongs to the youth ministry (i.e., the youth minister is hired to do "everything" in youth ministry.) They may also feel that you have to be a professional to work with youth.

A recruiting team enhances the effectiveness and credibility of the recruitment effort. This team can be comprised of two people from the youth ministry team—preferably one adult and one youth. Some youth ministry teams organize themselves into committees—worship, education, community, service, retreat. These committees can become recruiting teams for their particular programs.

The recruiting team should contact its prospects by phone and arrange personal meetings. It is a good idea to give team members the names of prospects they know personally and are more likely to be able to influence. The coordinator of youth ministry should be a part of a team contacting familiar prospects. Recruiters should be familiar with the direction of youth ministry, the various leadership positions, and what is involved in each position. Recruiters should have copies of the job descriptions and any other pertinent information about youth ministry. This is where a brochure containing all the leadership opportunities would be very helpful. Team members recruiting in pairs will feel more confident and more accountable for accomplishing their assigned tasks.

Recruiters should listen closely and be open to the realities of the individual situations of prospective leaders. Often recruiters from a church are interested only in the needs of the institution and fail to deal with real hindrances in the lives of prospective leaders. Positive concern with low pressure is the ideal recruiter's attitude.

Appeals may be made to many motives: service; personal relationships; gratitude for what one has been given; assistance to those carrying out the primary responsibility; utilization of personal gifts and abilities; opportunity to put one's faith into action; personal growth in knowledge, skill, and faith; influence over the lives of young people; teamwork; and other positive factors.

Recruiters will want to focus on reasons why the prospective leader is the best person they can think of for the position. Provide the prospect with several reasons, but do not give all the reasons. Hold some back to answer objections or hesitancies. And remember: It is a most significant opportunity and challenge, not something that will be very easy or require little effort.

Information is also necessary in a recruitment interview. You will need to share facts about the program in which you expect your prospective leader to work: time, place, numbers of people, types of activities, term of service, other leaders involved. You will also need to inform them about the plan for training, resources, support, and supervision.

With your recruiting teams, you might plan an interview with a prospective leader developed around the following framework:

Introduction: Be honest and challenging.

Appeal to motives: Draw out the best in the person.

Factual information: Tasks, time, and so on. Supply this in writing. Seek to discover the person's own view of the task.

Help they will receive: Training, resources, support, guidance, supervision.

Question: Will he or she accept the challenge? Express trust and confidence in the decision the person makes — whatever it is.

Conclusion: Ideally, invite to explore, train, or serve.

Above all, in your interview express enthusiasm for the church and youth ministry, for its mission, and for its effectiveness through dedicated persons.

Before recruiters make their calls, let each one have the experience of role playing a visit using the above outline as a guide. This will help to bolster the recruiters' confidence and to see any points that need more attention. The chart which follows is a visual summary of one way to handle recruiting.

Six Steps to Recruiting and Maintaining
a New Volunteer

6. Keep the Member Interested and on the Job

Give the volunteer a job that is interesting and important, yet one which will not take more time than he or she can give.

5. Sign on the Line

Get the person's time commitment and ask him or her to sign up.

4. Specific Proposal

Offer the job of his or her choice.

3. Discover a Preference

List the many volunteer jobs that make up the operation.

2. Arouse Interest

Stimulate curiosity about your program.

1. Contact

Find the person you want and arrange a meeting.

Recruiters not only must know the needs of the community; they also face the necessity of locating people who have time and interest to give in order to meet those needs.

The committee must ferret out and identify the person who must be called into service. Members of the committee must know the kinds of tasks to be performed, the time a volunteer can be expected to give, the time each job will take, and the satisfaction to be gained through service.

Trained recruiters and consistent recruiting is the answer to the need to enlist a sufficient number of citizens to carry on the responsibilities of any agency.[2]

Planning and providing exploration experiences for prospects

Help those prospects who are interested, but undecided or inexperienced, to become better acquainted with the area of their potential service. Provide written materials or other resources. Or plan and conduct an orientation session or course for several prospects. Or arrange for them to observe situations comparable to the one they might lead or to participate as an intern in such a setting.

Establishing agreements with leaders

Help each prospect come to a decision about the invitation to serve, and receive his or her response. If it is yes, agree together on placement in either a pre-service training opportunity or an actual leadership position if the person already possesses the abilities needed. And, using the job description, agree together on all terms of service. If desired, record this agreement as a contract and acknowledge and thank each new leader publicly. If his or her answer is no, record that decision, the reason for it, and any notes on future interests.

WORKSHEET 14: Identifying the Gifts of the Laity

Introduction

In helping laypeople to gain a vision of their universal calling to ministry in the world, there are several psychological barriers which must be overcome. Two of these barriers have to do with one's talents or "gifts."

The first attitude frequently expressed by laypeople is that God's work has always been done by "giants of the faith." Too frequently we have so romanticized these "giants" that they have taken on the aura of super people. A careful reading of both the Old and New Testaments will confirm the fact that throughout history God has done uncommon things through very common people. Our so-called Bible heroes frequently were reluctant, doubting, frightened people possessing no outstanding talents. It was the power of God working through them which made the difference. Lay people need to recognize this fact, and thereby recognize their own potential.

The second attitude has to do with our understanding of humility. While it is a virtue to be humble, too many Christian laypeople carry their concept of humility to the point of denying their own God-given talents. Despite the fact that the Apostle Paul highlights the importance of our gifts in the 12th Chapter of Romans, the 12th Chapter of I Corinthians, and elsewhere, too many laypeople depreciate their own gifts through a distorted sense of humility.

In an effort to help laypeople recognize their gifts and consider their potential for ministry, we frequently allocate a period of time at our *LAOS in Ministry* conferences for "gift identification." While there are a number of methods for helping people to identify their gifts, the *LAOS in Ministry* fellowship has found the following self-study to be especially useful. It is most helpful at conferences where participants are relative strangers to one another and are therefore not in a position to identify the gifts they see in others. Credit for this self-study goes to Richard Broholm of the Andover Newton Laity Project. We have made some revisions in his original design as a result of experience gained in our *LAOS in Ministry* retreats, but his basic approach is unchanged.

For best use, *Steps 1 and 2 should be presented on one sheet of paper, while Step 3, the Talent List, and Step 4 should be on a second sheet.* This is to prevent the talent list from influencing decisions made in the first two steps.

Identification of Gifts

Step 1:

Using the lines below write down a list of things which you have done in your life which you valued and/or enjoyed doing, no matter how small or insignificant you think they might appear to others. Try not to be influenced by what you think *others* would call valuable. This is what *you* value or enjoy. Go back in your childhood as far as you can. Try to list at least thirty things.

1. _____

2. _____

3. _____

4. _____

5. _____

6. _____

7. _____

8. _____

9. _____

10. _____

11. _____

12. _____

13. _____

14. _____

15. _____

16. _____

17. _____

18. _____

19. _____

20. _____

21. _____

22. _____

23. _____

24. _____

25. _____

26. _____

27. _____

28. _____

29. _____

30. _____

Step 2:

From your large list select the five which you value and/or enjoy the most and list them below:

1. _____

2. _____

3. _____

4. _____

5. _____

Step 3:

Think about the above list as accomplishments. Starting with the first accomplishment listed, recall step by step what you did. Refer to the following list of talents and put one small checkmark opposite each talent which you used in doing or making that accomplishment. If a talent comes to mind which is not listed, add it to the list and check it. When you have done this, go back over the list of checkmarks and determine which talent was the *most* important for the accomplishment, and put two more checkmarks on the line beside it. For the *second most important* talent put one additional checkmark on the line beside it.

Repeat the process for each of the five accomplishments.

A Talent List for the Identification of Gifts

Advise, counsel _____

Analyze, diagnose _____

Arbitrate, reconcile _____

Arrange _____

Artistic presentation _____

Audit, bookkeeping _____

Caretaking _____

Classify _____

Collect _____

Communicate _____

Compare _____

Commit myself _____

Compile _____

Compute _____

Construct, build _____

Coordinate _____

Conceptualize _____

Copy, record _____

Create _____

Demonstrate _____

Design, invent _____

Display _____

Drive _____

Do precision work _____

Encourage _____

Envision _____

Evaluate _____

Facilitate _____

Instruct, teach _____

Interpret _____

Lead _____

Learn _____

Listen _____

Love _____

Maintain _____

Manage _____

Make from instructions _____

Motivate, inspire _____

Negotiate _____

Observe _____

Organize _____

Perform _____

Persuade _____

Read _____

Repair _____

Research, investigate _____

Search for _____

Sell _____

Serve, wait on others _____

Supervise _____

Support _____

Talk _____

Use hands _____

Use tools _____

Write _____

Other: _____

Step 4:

Now add up the total number of checkmarks for each talent used. Identify your
most frequently used talent on the back side of this sheet. List the second most
frequently used talent, the third, fourth and fifth.

You have just identified your God-given "gifts."

STEP 4: Training Leaders

This step will help you organize your overall training strategy. It does not contain the information, skills, and techniques you need to become a trainer, but it does cover the steps you will need to take in organizing training programs for your adult leaders.

Orienting new leaders

Each newly enlisted leader needs to become familiar with the program in which he or she will serve — its goals, participants, history, and available resources. This may involve providing resource materials, counseling with individual members, arranging for observations, demonstrations, interviews, or participation as an intern or apprentice. An important ingredient in orientation is a general session for all new leaders. At this time the veteran leaders (adults and youth) can share the vision and direction of the youth ministry and look at the different programs with new leaders. Most new leaders will need more than an orientation to their leadership position — they will need pre-service training.

Diagnosing the needs of leaders

The key step in organizing a training program is to personalize it to meet the needs of the leaders. This will involve spending time to diagnose the learning needs of each leader. Here the job description with its list of needed abilities is helpful: What abilities does the leader already have? What can he or she learn "on the job"? Which will the leader need to develop through training and supervision?

This approach to training builds the training program around the special learning needs of the leaders, rather than designing a preset program for all your leaders. This individualized approach to training provides precisely what each leader needs for his or her leadership position. Using this approach, it becomes much easier to develop a plan of learning and even to combine the learning needs of several of your leaders. To assist each leader in the learning plan, a resource developed by Malcolm Knowles is included at the end of this chapter. It provides a very useful tool for the leader and for the coordinator or supervisor. It is an excellent way to monitor a person's progress.

Setting training goals

In setting goals with the leader you would do well to distinguish the various types of training opportunities. In *pre-service* training, the basic knowledge and skills needed before starting a job are presented. *In-service* training objectives offer opportunity for more specific knowledge and skills. Usually a leader's questions and learning needs will become the focus of in-service training. *Continuing education* opportunities are the general interest topics that do not necessarily relate to a specific job, but are engaged in for personal enrichment.

Once you have distinguished the type of training that needs to be provided and when it will be provided, you can assist the leader in setting goals for his or her learning, and guide them in a commitment to achieve these learning goals.

Worksheets are included at the end of this section to assist adult leaders in setting goals. The first one outlines six different types of behavioral outcomes and the most appropriate techniques that can be used in achieving those outcomes. Worksheet 15B provides a tool for developing specific objectives around the six types of behavioral outcomes.

Engaging leaders in training opportunities

The process of identifying training opportunities in relation to a person's training goals is an ongoing task. It is important to keep leaders informed about upcoming training events. It is also important to assist the leader's participation in training programs with funds for tuition, transportation, child care, and the like. After all you have done to enlist and secure this leader, be sure to care for these details. This oftentimes means the difference between a leader participating in training and not participating. Be sure to record and acknowledge each leader's participation in a training event. If you utilize Knowles' Learning Contract Form, you can appropriately record the completion of a learning objective.

Locating and planning opportunities for training

Based on the leaders' needs and training goals, locate the existing training opportunities which will help leaders to reach their goals: resource materials, diocesan/parish-sponsored training programs, adult religious education courses, college and community-based courses, guided study programs, resource persons. Where training is not available, develop it: workshops, courses, observation, demonstration, guided study, internships. When appropriate, these training events should be sponsored in cooperation with other parishes.

The coordinator of youth ministry is not responsible for doing all the training, but rather for providing training to meet the learning needs of the leaders. There are usually a large number of training programs available for your leaders that you can take advantage of. Most dioceses across the country provide annual religious education or youth ministry conferences. These make marvelous training events. If the coordinator sat down with all leaders and helped them choose workshops based on their individual learning needs, the conference could become an integral part of your overall training plan. This is but one example of utilizing an existing training event for your purposes.

The coordinator who is qualified and interested in designing training programs will find it useful to consult "A Guide for Designing a Training Program," by Cyril R. Mill, in *Activities for Trainers: Fifty Useful Designs* (La Jolla, CA: University Associates, 1980).

WORKSHEET 15A: Matching Techniques to Desired Behavioral Outcomes

Type of Behavioral Outcome	Most Appropriate Techniques
Knowledge (Generalizations about experience; internalization of information)	Lecture, television, debate, dialog, interview, symposium, panel, group interview, colloquy, motion picture, slide film, recording, book-based discussion, reading.
Understanding (Application of information and generalizations)	Audience participation, demonstration, motion picture, dramatization, Socratic discussion, problem-solving discussion, case discussion, critical incident process, case method, games.
Skills (Incorporation of new ways of performing through practice)	Role playing . . . games, action mazes, participative cases, T-Group, nonverbal exercises, skill practice exercises, drill, coaching.
Attitudes (Adoption of new feelings through experiencing greater success with them than with old)	Experience-sharing discussion, group-centered discussion, role playing, critical incident process, case method, games, participative cases, T-Group, nonverbal exercises.
Values (The adoption and priority arrangement of beliefs)	Television, lecture, (sermon), debate, dialog, symposium, colloquy, motion picture, dramatization, guided discussion, experience-sharing discussion, role playing, critical incident process, games, T-Group.
Interests (Satisfying exposure to new activities)	Television, demonstration, motion picture, slide film, dramatization, experience-sharing discussion, exhibits, trips, nonverbal exercises.

WORKSHEET 15B: Stating Learning Objectives

Behavioral Outcome		Specific Content Areas
To develop	1.	
knowledge about _____	2.	
_____	3.	
_____	4.	
	5.	
	6.	
	7.	
To develop	1.	
understanding of _____	2.	
_____	3.	
_____	4.	
	5.	
	6.	
	7.	
To develop	1.	
skills in_____	2.	
_____	3.	
_____	4.	
	5.	
	6.	
	7.	
To develop	1.	
attitudes toward _____	2.	
_____	3.	
_____	4.	
	5.	
	6.	
	7.	
To develop	1.	
values of _____	2.	
_____	3.	
_____	4.	
	5.	
	6.	
	7.	

To develop	1.
interest in _____	2.
_____	3.
_____	4.
	5.
	6.
	7.

STEP 5: Supporting Leaders

Now that you have worked so hard to recruit, place, and train your leaders, you will want to hold onto them, help them learn from their ministry, and get them to return next year. By developing the supervision and support functions of your leader development system, you will be working on these crucial issues. Supervision and support may be the two most overlooked elements in a parish youth ministry leader development system. To overcome this problem, study and plan around the following tasks.

Authorizing leaders to begin service

Leaders need a formal way to begin their ministry with youth. You can authorize the beginning of their service through a formal worship service. For several years now Catechist Sunday has been a formal time at Sunday Eucharist to authorize the ministry of the catechists. This formal commissioning serves to authorize leaders for their ministry. In a public way these leaders are recognized by the community and blessed. A similar ceremony can enhance the recognized status of pastoral youth ministry.

Developing relationships between leaders and supervisors

For each leader designate a supervisor—someone who will support and guide the leader in ways that will help him or her to improve in leadership. Help leader and supervisor develop an initial agreement regarding their relationship and responsibilities. They should plan to communicate regularly, openly, and with mutual trust. The supervisor may be the coordinator of youth ministry, a youth ministry team member, or a member of the parish staff (e.g., the DRE may supervise the catechists in the youth ministry program).

This is the time to remember the concepts of leadership that were presented in chapter 2, especially the dynamics of situational leadership. Be aware of the fact that new volunteers need and appreciate *direction* regarding tasks and structures. When they gain knowledge and motivation, these tasks can be more easily *delegated* to them. Also, volunteers need the right amount of *relationship support*—not too much early on, high relational support as they get into the swing of things, and less relational support when they are seasoned volunteers and can handle delegation.

Engaging leaders in support-guidance groups

In addition, help each leader participate in a group which supports and guides him or her as a person and a leader. This may involve gathering adult leaders in the youth ministry or in a particular program to share their experiences, reflect on what they are learning, and ask the group for guidance. Many youth ministry leaders schedule these meetings into the calendar for the year, making it a regular part of the job description and commitment. Oftentimes the adult support group meets in lieu of the regular youth program. Many times these support-guidance groups become occasions for shared prayer and reflection on the Scriptures and Christian tradition. At other times they become adult education groups seeking to explore more deeply questions of theology and spirituality.

Some distinctions between the different goals of support groups can be helpful to people who are planning to start or join such a group.

First of all, it is important to clarify whether the members of the support group are expecting a *personal growth* experience, or a *professional ministry focus* on issues and skills. While all successful groups have a human side that meets personal needs, support groups function best if everyone agrees that the primary goals will be related to ministry (or the professional field of interest to the group). This is vital because most groups cannot fulfill both agendas simultaneously, and split expectations can create tension and drain energy.

The immediate goal of a support group is learning and encouragement for its members, which can fall into three broad categories: (1) *New ideas*—Stimulation, challenge, and the exchange of insights or information result from the dialogue of colleagues. (2) *Concrete help*—Working together to solve problems gives members a chance to try out new methods, skills, and suggestions. (3) *Personal support*—The support group is a safe place for members to share disappointments or successes so that they can feel linked to their peers with confidence and enthusiasm.

As a long-range goal, support groups have the purpose of improving the quality of youth ministry. Because these groups continue, past and future members have a network of associates to contact for greater effectiveness in their field. Over time, the development of support groups should enhance the commitment and quality of persons dedicated to ministry.

Helping leaders engage in the parish, community, and world

Still another form of supervision is provided through the leaders' participation in wider circles of responsibility: liturgical, social, catechetical, administrative, or community ministries of the local parish as well as the life of the surrounding community and world. Help leaders engage in and profit by such experiences. Involvement in the broader parish, community, and world helps to enrich not only the leader, but also the youth ministry.

Providing the information and resources which leaders need

Through each leader's supervisor, supply whatever standard and optional resources and other information the leader needs. In addition, provide a library or learning resource center. Such a center should have resources for both the personal and spiritual growth of the leaders and for conducting their ministry. Resources should include books, periodicals of interest and importance, youth resource materials (e.g., texts and youth periodicals), cassette programs, and audiovisual resources.

Gathering information about and evaluating leaders' work

Each leader and supervisor gathers information about the leader's work through observation, consultation, group discussion, instruments, or other means. On this basis they weigh the leader's actual performance against the goals of the program and the criteria of the job description. (You may also keep a cumulative record of each leader's training involvement and evaluation.)

Guiding leaders in planning and improving their work

The supervisor uses information from the evaluation as he or she guides the leader in planning for personal and ministerial growth. Each leader is helped to diagnose needs and set goals for in-service training.

Expressing and celebrating the support of the Church

We encourage all concerned to express gratitude, appreciation, and support for all leaders in youth ministry. Periodically we celebrate this support in more formal ways, as in community worship or special recognition. And of course, we express appreciation to each leader at the conclusion of his or her service. We may express and celebrate support through parties and dinners throughout the year, especially through an annual evening of recognition. This evening of recognition might include a dinner (perhaps prepared by the young people themselves), entertainment, and some sign of appreciation (e.g., a book, certificate of appreciation, handmade gift). There should also be some recognition of those who have given five years of service to youth. Expressing and celebrating this recognition is very important. Too often we take our leaders for granted, and then wonder why they do not return. Show them how special they are!

RESOURCE: Some Guidelines for the Use of Learning Contracts in Field-Based Learning

Why Use Learning Contracts?

One of the most significant findings from research about adult learning (e.g., Allen Tough's *The Adult's Learning Projects,* Ontario Institute for Studies in Education, Toronto, 1971) is that when adults go about learning something naturally (as contrasted with being taught something) they are highly self-directing. Evidence is beginning to accumulate, too, that what adults learn on their own initiative they learn more deeply and permanently than what they learn by being taught.

Those kinds of learning that are engaged in for purely personal development can perhaps be planned and carried out completely by an individual on his or her own terms and with only a loose structure. But those kinds of learning that have as their purpose improving one's competence to perform in a job or in a profession must take into account the needs and expectations of organizations, professions, and society. Learning contracts provide a means for negotiating a reconciliation between these external needs and expectations, and the learner's internal needs and interests.

Furthermore, in traditional education the learning activity is structured by the teacher and the institution. The learner is told what objectives he or she is to work toward, what resources to use and how (and when) to use them, and how accomplishment of the objectives will be evaluated. This imposed structure conflicts with the adult's deep psychological need to be self-directing and may induce resistance, apathy, or withdrawal. Learning contracts provide a vehicle for making the planning of learning experiences a mutual undertaking between a learner and the learner's helper, mentor, teacher, and often, peers. By participating in the process of diagnosing needs, formulating objectives, identifying resources, choosing strategies, and evaluating accomplishments, the learner develops a sense of ownership of and commitment to the plan.

Finally, in field-based learning particularly, there is a strong possibility that what is to be learned from the experience will be less clear to both the learner and the field supervisor than what work is to be done. There is a long tradition of field-experience learners being exploited for the performance of menial tasks. The learning contract is a means for making the *learning objectives* of the field experience clear and explicit for both the learner and the field supervisor.

How Do You Develop a Learning Contract?

Step 1: Diagnose Your Learning Needs. A learning need is the gap between where you are now and where you want to be in regard to a particular set of competencies.

You may already be aware of certain learning needs as a result of a personal appraisal process or the long accumulation of evidence for yourself of the gaps between where you are now and where you would like to be.

If not (or even if so), it might be worth your while to go through this process: First, construct a model of the competencies required to excellently perform · the role (e.g., parent, teacher, civic leader, manager, consumer, professional worker, etc.) you are concerned about. There may be a competency model already in existence that you can use as a thought-starter and checklist; many professions are developing such models. If not, you can build your own with help from friends, colleagues, supervisors, and expert resource people. A competency can be thought of as the ability to do something at some level of proficiency, and is usually composed of some combination of knowledge, understanding, skill, attitude, and values. For example, "ability to ride a bicycle from my home to the store" is a competency that involves some knowledge of how a bicycle operates and the route to the store; an understanding of some of the dangers inherent in riding a bicycle; skill in mounting, pedaling, steering, and stopping a bicycle; an attitude of desire to ride a bicycle; and a valuing of the exercise it will yield. "Ability to ride a bicycle in a cross-country race" would be a higher-level competency that would require greater knowledge, understanding, and skill. It is useful to produce a competency model even if it is crude and subjective because of the clearer sense of direction it will give you.

Having constructed a competency model, your next task is to assess the gap between where you are now and where the model says you should be in regard to each competency. You can do this alone or with the help of people who have been observing your performance. The chances are that you will find that you have already developed some competencies to a level of excellence, so that you can concentrate on those you have not. An example of a part of a competency model showing how needs have been diagnosed is shown below.

Step 2: Specify Your Learning Objectives. You are now ready to start filling out the first column of the learning contract, "Learning objectives." Each of the learning needs diagnosed in Step 1 should be translated into a learning objective. Be sure that your objectives describe what you will *learn*. (For example, "To read the following books . . ." is not a learning objective; a learning objective will describe what you want to learn from those books. State them in terms that are most meaningful to you—content acquisition, terminal behaviors, or directions of growth.)

Step 3: Specify Learning Resources and Strategies. When you have finished listing your objectives, move over to the second column of the contract, "Learning resources and strategies," and describe how you propose to go about accomplishing *each* objective. Identify the resources (material and human) you plan to use in your field experience and the strategies (techniques and tools) you will employ in making use of them. Here is an example:

Learning objective	Learning resources and strategies
Improve my ability to organize my work efficiently so that I can accomplish 20 percent more work in a day.	1. Find books and articles in the library on how to organize my work and manage time, and read them. 2. Interview three executives on how they organize their work, then observe them for one day each, noting techniques they use. 3. Select the best techniques from each, plan a day's work, and have a colleague observe me for a day, giving me feedback.

Step 4: Specify Target Dates. This column provides a self-disciplining device that enables you to schedule your time more efficiently by specifying target dates for completing each of your learning objectives.

Step 5: Specify Evidence of Accomplishment. After completing the third column, move over to the fourth column, "Evidence of accomplishment of objectives," and describe what evidence you will collect to indicate the degree to which you have achieved each objective. Perhaps the following examples of evidence for different types of objectives will stimulate your thinking about what evidence you might accumulate.

Type of objective	Examples of evidence
Knowledge	Reports of knowledge acquired, as in essays, examinations, oral presentations, audiovisual presentations, annotated bibliographies.
Understanding	Examples of utilization of knowledge in solving problems, as in action projects, research projects with conclusions and recommendations, plans for curriculum change, etc.
Skills	Performance exercises, videotaped performances with ratings by observers.
Attitudes	Attitudinal rating scales; performance in real situations, role playing, simulation games, critical incident cases, and so on, with feedback from participants and/or observers.
Values	Value rating scales; performance in value clarification groups, critical incident cases, simulation exercises, and so on, with feedback from participants and/or observers.

Step 6: Specify How the Evidence Will Be Validated. After you have specified what evidence you will gather for each objective in column four, move over to column five, "Criteria and means for validating evidence." For each objective first specify what criteria you propose the evidence will be judged by. The criteria will vary according to the type of objective. For example, appropriate criteria for knowledge objectives might include comprehensiveness, depth, precision, clarity, authentication, usefulness, and scholarliness. For skill objectives, more appropriate criteria may be poise, speed, flexibility, gracefulness, precision, and imaginativeness. After you have specified the criteria, indicate the means you propose to use to have the evidence judged according to these criteria. For example, if you produce a paper or report, who will you have read it and what are their qualifications? Will they express their judgments by rating scales, descriptive reports, evaluative reports? One of the actions that helps to differentiate "distinguished" from "adequate" performance in self-directed learning is the wisdom with which a learner selects his or her validators.

Step 7: Review Your Contract with Consultants. After you have completed the first draft of your contract you will find it useful to review it with two or three friends, supervisors, or other expert resource people to get their reactions and suggestions. Here are some questions you might have them ask about the contract to get optimal benefit from their help:

- Are the learning objectives clear, understandable, and realistic; do they describe what you propose to learn?
- Can they think of other objectives you might consider?
- Do the learning strategies and resources seem reasonable, appropriate, and efficient?
- Can they think of other resources and strategies you might consider?
- Does the evidence seem relevant to the various objectives, and would it convince them?
- Can they suggest other evidence you might consider?
- Are the criteria and means for validating the evidence clear, relevant, and convincing?
- Can they think of other ways to validate the evidence that you might consider?

Step 8: Carry Out the Contract. You now simply do what the contract calls for. But keep in mind that as you work on it you may find that your notions about what you want to learn and how you want to learn it may change. So don't hesitate to revise your contract as you go along.

Step 9: Evaluate Your Learning. When you have completed your contract you will want to get some assurance that you have in fact learned what you set out to learn. Perhaps the simplest way to do this is to ask the consultants you used in step 6 to examine your evidence and validation data and give you their judgment about their adequacy.

Learning Contract Form

Learner _____ Learning experience _____

Learning objectives	Learning resources and strategies	Target date for completion	Evidence of accomplishment of objectives	Criteria and means for validating evidence

Putting It All Together

Now we come to the payoff. It is time to decide what your own system for leader development will look like. Based on your study of the system outlined in this chapter and on your own evaluation of your present work, you can now plot out the overall design for the work that must be done.

How will you go about deciding? Be sure to work with your youth ministry team. Here are some sources of help:

- Your own past experience in enlisting, training, and supervising leaders.
- Your notes on the tasks outlined in this chapter.
- Your use of the assessment procedures in chapter 8 and the analysis and recommendations you made at that point.
- Your investigation of what other parishes are doing to develop leaders.
- Your reading of other resources in leader development.
- Your use of resource persons from your diocese, colleges, or community agencies.

If you choose to use the self-reflection questions found at the end of this chapter, the data you will generate will help you in designing your own system. If you prefer you can sketch your design as an outline. Use the major functions and outline the process and major tasks you have set for yourself. The important thing is to get it down in a systematic way so that you can see all its parts and the way it will work as a whole.

Go to it!

Two Conclusions

First, even though you did not get into youth ministry to spend major portions of your time designing and managing a leader system, the work and time spent creating your own system will return many benefits in the long run. By developing adult and youth leaders, you, the coordinator of youth ministry, will create precious time for attending to the aspects of your youth ministry that only you can do. Your leader development system will return to you a most precious gift—more time to devote to young people. *Be patient with the process!*

Second, *adapt . . . adapt . . . adapt!* Make the system work for you. Any leader development system is intended to serve as a guide—create your own, using the materials in this book and in other resource books. It has to work for *you!*

Reflection Questions on Leadership Development

Since the leadership system presented in this book is a general model, it will have to be adapted in order to suit your particular situation. The reflection questions which follow are designed to help you or the youth ministry team as a whole to think about how you can use this material.

General

Take a moment to consider whether the five steps of the leadership development system make sense to you and whether they are appropriate for your congregation.

1) The strengths of this system seem to be . . .
2) The weaknesses of this system seem to be . . .
3) Is there any major function which you would eliminate as unnecessary?
4) Is there any function which is not included here and which you would add?

Enlisting leaders

1) What are the ways in which you currently enlist leaders?
2) How are you currently interpreting youth ministry as an opportunity for Christian leadership?
3) Which of the options suggested in Step 2 seems best suited to your situation?
4) What concrete steps will you take to begin interpreting the leadership needs of youth ministry to the community? List some approaches that you will try.
5) List the various ways in which you can help to recruit leaders.
6) Who will assist you in the task of searching for potential leaders? (This is a real opportunity for your team to be involved.)

7) What tasks do you and/or your team need to do so that you can develop a list of potential leaders?

8) Which approach to developing a file of potential leaders is best suited to your situation? Are there other approaches better suited to your needs?

9) What steps will you take to implement a filing system?

10) What procedure will you use in matching leadership needs and potential leaders?

11) What possibilities exist if you have any "excess" of leadership resources?

12) How will you go about discovering the potential leadership resources within your community? List some of the community organizations, agencies, and personnel who would be helpful to a youth ministry.

Training leaders

1) Here are several questions to consider in planning an orientation program for new leaders: (a) Who will be attending? (b) What are the needs and expectations? (c) What do you want to happen? (d) How will your design allow this to happen? (e) Will you provide written materials concerning the youth ministry?

2) What approach will you take to diagnose the needs of your leaders?

3) Will you be able to meet individually with your leaders to diagnose their needs for learning? If not, how will you go about diagnosing their needs for learning?

4) Will you be able to adapt Knowles' Learning Contract process for use in your leader development system?

5) How will you utilize the three types of training opportunities (pre-service, in-service, and continuing education) in planning training opportunities around the learning needs of your leaders?

6) Will you be able to meet individually with your leaders to set training goals based on their learning needs? If not, how will you go about helping your leaders set training goals?

7) To assist you in locating existing training opportunities, consider the following sources: (a) What training opportunities are offered by particular diocesan agencies: school, office, youth ministry office, religious education office? (b) What diocesan or regional conferences are offered that you can take advantage of? (c) Does your diocese offer catechist training courses, youth ministry training courses, or adult education courses that you can take advantage of? (d) Are there local community colleges or universities that offer continuing education courses or workshops that you can take advantage of? (e) Are there community agencies which offer seminars, workshops, and courses relating to youth concerns? (f) What agencies have developed speaker lists from which you can select resource

people to assist you in providing training? (These lists are developed by dioceses, councils of churches, community agencies, and so on) (g) What training opportunities exist in other churches which you can take advantage of? (h) Have you contacted other parishes/congregations in your area concerning their youth ministry training opportunities?

Supporting leaders

1) What procedure/service will you develop to formally authorize your leaders as they begin their service in youth ministry?

2) Have you identified a supervisor for each of your leaders?

3) How regularly will the supervisor and leader meet?

4) What areas of the leader's ministry will they discuss?

5) What approaches will you use in providing your leaders with support?

6) Will you integrate support-guidance groups into your regular schedule?

7) What other involvements will you suggest to your leaders in the parish/congregation and in the community/world?

8) What type of print and audio-visual resources will you provide for your leaders to use in their work?

9) What resources exist in your parish/congregation and in your surrounding community that could assist your leaders in their work?

10) What periodicals does your parish/congregation subscribe to that would be useful to your leaders? To what periodicals do your public library and diocesan office subscribe that would be useful to your leaders?

11) What approach(s) will you take in gathering information about each leader's performance?

12) How will you guide each leader in using the information to improve his or her ministry?

13) What are the ways in which you, as the coordinator, will express the gratitude and support of the church for the youth ministry leaders?

14) Will you plan these different styles of support into your regular schedule?

Notes

1. Marlene Wilson, *The Effective Management of Volunteer Programs* (Boulder, CO: Volunteer Management Associates, 1976), pp. 115–118.

2. Ibid., p. 120.

A Youth Ministry Library for $300

The resources listed below are suggested for your consideration when developing a youth ministry resource library for your adult and youth leaders. These resources have been selected because they meet several or all of the following criteria:

- Fundamental—The book presents basic knowledge and skills necessary for volunteer leaders.
- Flexible—The resource contains a variety of material which can be used in a variety of programs by volunteer leaders.
- Enduring—Most of the resources listed will not become obsolete in a year or two.
- Tested—The resource has been found useful by other youth ministers and/or the staff of the Northeast Center.
- Inexpensive—The resources listed are all paperbacks; no audiovisual resources are suggested due to their cost. The entire list of resources adds up to approximately $300.

General Theology

Hellwig, Monica. *Understanding Catholicism*. New York: Paulist Press, 1981. Optional. $5.00.
Killgallon, J., M. O'Shaugnessy, and G. Weber. *Becoming Catholic—Even If You Happen to Be One*. Chicago: ACTA Foundation, 1980. Optional. $4.50.
McBrien, Richard. *Catholicism*. Study ed. Minneapolis: Winston Press, 1981. $25.00.

Youth Ministry—In General

Harris, Maria. *A Portrait of Youth Ministry*. New York: Paulist Press, 1981. $8.00.
Warren, Michael. *Youth and the Future of the Church*. New York: Seabury Press, 1982. $10.95.

Youth Ministry Manuals and Handbooks

Clapp, Steve, and Jerry O. Cook. *Youth Workers' Handbook*. Champaign, IL: C–4 Resources, 1981. Write to: C–4 Resources, P.O. Box 1408, Champaign, IL 61820. $12.00.
Coleman, Bill, and Patty Coleman. *CYM's First Youth Ministry Handbook*. Mystic,

CT: Growth Associates, 1980–81. Write to: Growth Associates, 22 Willow Street, Mystic, CT 06355. $8.00.

Coleman, Lyman. *Handbook of Serendipity.* Littleton, CO: Serendipity House, 1980. Write to: Serendipity House, Box 1012, Littleton, CO 80160. $5.00.

Corbett, Jan. *Creative Youth Leadership.* Valley Forge, PA: Judson Press, 1977. $4.95.

Holderness, Ginny Ward. *Youth Ministry: The New Team Approach.* Atlanta: John Knox Press, 1981. $10.00.

Ludwig, Glen. *Building an Effective Youth Ministry.* Nashville: Abingdon Press, 1979. $4.95.

Rice, Wayne, John Roberto, and Mike Yaconelli, eds. *Creative Resources for Youth Ministry.* Six-vol. series. Winona, MN: Saint Mary's Press, 1982. $9.00 per vol. Titles:
- *Creative Learning Experiences*
- *Creative Communication and Community Building*
- *Creative Projects and Worship Experiences*
- *Creative Gaming 1*
- *Creative Gaming 2*
- *Creative Gaming 3*

Sparks, Lee, ed. *The Youth Group How-To Book: 66 Practical Projects and Programs to Help You Build a Better Youth Group.* Loveland, CO: Group Books, 1981. $14.95.

Youth Experiential Annual Resource. Champaign, IL: C–4 Resources, 1981. Write to: C–4 Resources, P.O. Box 1408, Champaign, IL 61820. $12.00.

Counseling

Gordon, Thomas. *Teacher Effectiveness Training.* New York: Wyden, 1974. $6.95.

Kennedy, Eugene. *On Becoming a Counselor.* New York: Seabury Press, 1977. $8.95.

Justice and Peace

Mische, Gerald, and Patricia Mische. *Toward a Human World Order.* New York: Paulist Press, 1977. $3.95.

O'Hare, Padraic, ed. *Education for Peace and Justice.* New York: Harper & Row, 1983. $9.95.

Wallis, Jim. *The Call to Conversion.* New York: Harper & Row, 1981. $6.95.

Leadership

Johnson, Douglas. *The Care and Feeding of Volunteers.* Nashville: Abingdon Press, 1976. $4.95.

Keating, Charles. *The Leadership Book.* Rev. ed. New York: Paulist Press, 1983. $4.95.
Rauner, Judy. *Helping People Volunteer.* San Diego: Marlborough Publications, 1980.
Write to: Marlborough Publications, P.O. Box 16406, San Diego, CA 92116.
$13.00.

Prayer

Link, Mark. *Breakaway.* Allen, TX: Argus Communications, 1980. $3.25.
———— . *You.* Allen, TX: Argus Communications, 1976. $2.95.

Religious Education

Groome, Thomas. *Christian Religious Education.* San Francisco: Harper & Row, 1980.
$10.95.
Harris, Maria. *DRE Book.* New York: Paulist Press, 1976. $4.95.
Seymour, Jack L., and Donald E. Miller. *Contemporary Approaches to Christian Education.* Nashville: Abingdon Press, 1982. $6.95.
Westerhoff, John. *Will Our Children Have Faith?* New York: Seabury Press, 1976.
$6.95.

Retreats

Nelson, Virgil, and Lynn Nelson. *The Retreat Handbook.* Valley Forge, PA: Judson
Press, 1976. $5.95.
Reichter, Arlo, et al. *The Group Retreat Book.* Loveland, CO: Group Books, 1983.
$15.95.

Service

Campolo, Anthony. *Ideas for Social Action.* El Cajon, CA: Youth Specialties, 1983.
$6.00.
Kohler, Mary Conway. *Young People Learning to Care.* New York: Seabury Press,
1983. $7.95.
Schultjann, Marie. *Ministry of Service: A Manual for Social Involvement.* New York:
Paulist Press, 1976. $1.95.

Sociology/Psychology

DiGiacomo, James, and Edward Wakin. *Understanding Teenagers.* Allen, TX: Argus
Communications, 1983. $5.95.
Farel, Anita. *Early Adolescence and Religion.* Carrboro, NC: Center for Early Adolescence, 1982. Write to: Center for Early Adolescence, Suite 223, Carr Mill Mall,
Carrboro, NC 27510. $5.00.

Hill, John. *Understanding Early Adolescence.* Carrboro, NC: Center for Early Adolescence, 1981. $4.00.
Strommen, Merton. *Five Cries of Youth.* New York: Harper & Row, 1979. $4.95.

Teaching

Griggs, Donald. *Teaching Teachers to Teach.* Nashville: Abingdon Press, 1974. $5.95.
Reichert, Richard. *A Learning Process for Religious Education.* Dayton, OH: Pflaum Press, 1975. $4.95.

Worship

Mossi, John P., ed. *Modern Liturgy Handbook.* New York: Paulist Press, 1976. $6.95.
Searle, Mark. *Liturgy Made Simple.* Collegeville, MN: Liturgical Press, 1981. $2.95.
Walsh, Eugene, *The Theology of Celebration.* Glendale, AZ: Pastoral Arts Associates of North America, 1977. $1.25.

ACKNOWLEDGMENTS continued:

Worksheet 7 entitled "Leader Development in Youth Ministry" (pages 107–111) is adapted from *Designing Your System for Leader Development,* by George E. Koehler. Copyright © 1972 by the Board of Education, The United Methodist Church. Reproduced by permission of Discipleship Resources, P.O. Box 840, Nashville, TN 37202.

Worksheet 14 entitled "Identifying the Gifts of the Laity" (pages 138–141) is from an article by William E. Diehl in *Laity Exchange,* © 1980 by the Lutheran Church in America. Reproduced with permission.

The resource entitled "Some Guidelines for the Use of Learning Contracts in Field-Based Learning" (pages 151–155) is reproduced from *The Modern Practice of Adult Education,* copyright 1980 by Malcolm S. Knowles. Published by Cambridge, The Adult Education Company, 888 Seventh Avenue, New York, New York 10106. Reproduced with the permission of the publisher.

Photos: John Arms, 56; AT&T Photo Service, 134; Ron Engh, 16, 60; Michael Goldberg, 10, 34; Jack Hamilton, 24, 52, 66, 98, 116, 119, 128, 143; Jean-Claude LeJeune, cover, 42, 156; Ron Sievert, 104.